POP CULTURE

American

from The Ten Commandments
to Twilight

DANIEL BENJAMIN

Cavendish
Square

New York

Published in 2014 by Cavendish Square Publishing, LLC
303 Park Avenue South, Suite 1247, New York, NY 10010

Website: cavendishsq.com

This publication represents the opinions and views of the author based on his or her personal experience, knowledge, and research. The information in this book serves as a general guide only. The author and publisher have used their best efforts in preparing this book and disclaim liability rising directly or indirectly from the use and application of this book.

CPSIA Compliance Information: Batch #WS13CSQ

All websites were available and accurate when this book was sent to press.

Library of Congress Cataloging-in-Publication Data

Benjamin, Daniel. • American life and movies from The Ten Commandments to Twilight /
Dan Elish ; editors, Michelle Bisson, Bethany Larson.
p. cm. — (Pop culture)
Summary:"Provides a comprehensive look at the history of film in America"—Provided by publisher.
Includes bibliographical references and index.
ISBN 978-1-60870-921-2 (hardcover)—ISBN 978-1-62712-121-7 (paperback)
—ISBN 978-1-60870-926-7 (ebook)
1. Motion pictures—United States—History—20th century—Juvenile literature.
2. Motion pictures—United States—History—21st century—Juvenile literature. I. Title.
PN1993.5.U6E335 2012 • 791.430973—dc23 • 2011045889

Editors: Michelle Bisson, Bethany Larson • Art Director: Anahid Hamparian
Series Designer: Alicia Mikles • Photo research by Lindsay Aveilhe

The photographs in this book are used by permission and through the courtesy of:
Cover photo courtesy of Everett Collection and AF archive/Alamy. AF archive/Alamy: p. 4; Bettmann/ Corbis: p. 6, 9; Everett Collection: p. 13; Pictorial Press Ltd/Alamy: p. 15; Anthony Cake/Photoshot/Getty Images: p. 17; AF archive/Alamy: p. 18; AP Photo: p. 22; United Artists/Getty Images: p. 29; Photos 12/ Alamy: p. 31; Everett Collection: p. 32; AF archive/Alamy: p. 35; AP Photo: p. 40; Kobal Collection: p. 43; AF archive/Alamy: p. 46, 48, 50; Dennis Brack/Newscom: p. 56; AF archive/Alamy: p. 58, 60; Pictorial Press Ltd/Alamy: p. 65; Photos 12/Alamy: p. 67; Reuters/Corbis: p. 72; AF archive/Alamy: p. 74; Frank Trapper/ Sygma/Corbis: p. 78; Everett Collection: p. 81; Doug Kanter/AFP/Getty Images: p. 86; AF archive/Alamy: p. 88, 90; Pictorial Press Ltd/Alamy: p. 92; AF archive/Alamy: p. 94, 96, 97;Photos 12/Alamy: p. 99.

Printed in the United States of America

Contents

On the Waterfront tells the timely and timeless tale of the "one just man" who resists peer pressure in favor of the larger cause of unveiling injustice.

Introduction

ALTHOUGH FILM IS A YOUNG MEDIUM— especially when compared to music or books, which have influenced culture for centuries—it is a powerful tool for storytelling. Over the past sixty years, film has emerged as the art form that seems to hold the most sway over American popular culture. *On the Waterfront* (1954), *Mary Poppins* (1964), *Dr. Strangelove* (1964), *Easy Rider* (1969), *Jaws* (1975), *Star Wars* (1977), *When Harry Met Sally . . .* (1989), *Titanic* (1997), *Avatar* (2009)—these films and many others tell stories that captivate, amuse, and resonate with audiences.

Many movies are made to entertain as many people as possible; others are conceived to comment on a particular popular trend or historical event. But whatever the filmmaker's intent, all movies hold up a mirror to the times in which they were made. Since the 1950s, movies have not only told entertaining stories, but have analyzed and reflected certain historical events and trends in American culture in a way that allows these subjects to be seen in a new light. Whether dramatic, comedic, or thought-provoking, the movie industry mirrors changes and trends in culture and society, and vice versa.

Even the rich were hit in the Great Depression of 1929. Here, a Wall Street investor down on his luck tries to sell his luxury car after losing all his money when the stock market crashed that October.

ONE

1950s:

Trouble Brewing Beneath the American Dream

THE 1930S AND 1940S WERE VERY DIFFICULT decades for the United States. In October 1929, the stock market crashed and led to the Great Depression, the worst economic crisis in the nation's history. A little more than a decade later, the United States found itself in the middle of World War II, fighting against Germany and Italy in Europe and Japan in the Pacific. Understandably, once that war was won, most Americans were eager to enjoy themselves. Veterans married and moved to the suburbs en masse to pursue the American dream: a home, car, and community with good schools for their children to attend.

On the one hand, the 1950s was a decade of great prosperity. With the economy humming again, many families—at least many white families—were able to live on one income. Fathers went to work while moms stayed home and took care of the kids and the household. But brewing beneath the surface of this seeming suburban paradise were signs of the issues that would bubble up to the surface a decade later—including the civil rights and women's movements—to show that all was not well with the American dream, Fittingly, American movies of the decade reflected both the optimism of a nation that had survived the Depression and won a major world war, and the fearful insecurity of a country that was dealing with big changes both at home and abroad.

COMMUNISM AND THE BIBLICAL EPIC

Though the United States had helped win World War II, peacetime brought new fears to the country. Beginning in 1950, many Americans became unduly worried about the influence of communist ideology in the United States. In 1950, Wisconsin senator Joseph McCarthy claimed that he had a list of "members of the Communist Party and members of a spy ring" who worked in the State Department. Though McCarthy was never able to prove any of his claims, many Americans who were terrified of the Soviet Union's broadening influence in the world as well as the possible use of atomic and hydrogen bombs believed in and supported his witch hunt.

While McCarthy had the nation's ear, thousands of loyal American citizens were falsely accused of being communists and fired from their jobs. Today, the term *McCarthyism* refers to the political attitudes of those seeking to identify communists by coercing accusations of treason or disloyalty. Perhaps the best-known example of McCarthyism came from Hollywood.

In 1947, a group of studio executives made a blacklist or a roster of people not to associate with or hire. It named hundreds of writers, actors, and directors who were alleged communist sympathizers. Eleven people on the list were called to testify before the House Un-American Activities Committee (HUAC). Ten of them, dubbed the "Hollywood Ten," refused to appear because they believed the hearing was unconstitutional and violated their First Amendment rights. They were then all charged with contempt of Congress and proceedings against them began in the U.S. House of Representatives.

A group of Hollywood stars, led by Humphrey Bogart, went to Washington, D.C., in 1947, to protest the HUAC hearings, to no avail. They were (*front row, left to right*): Geraldine Brooks, June Havoc, Marsha Hunt, Lauren Bacall, Richard Conte, and Evelyn Keyes; (*back row, left to right*): Paul Henreid, Humphrey Bogart, Gene Kelly, and Danny Kaye.

On November 24, the House found the "Hollywood Ten" guilty of contempt of Congress. Additionally, the Motion Picture Association of America released a statement that the Hollywood Ten would be suspended or fired from their jobs and would not be reemployed until each of them publicly renounced communism or were cleared of the contempt charges. The members of the Hollywood Ten each spent one year in prison. They appealed their convictions, but all were found guilty. The cases were eventually appealed to the Supreme Court, which denied review of the case.

Dalton Trumbo, one of the most famous of the Ten, had his screenwriting credit for *Roman Holiday* reinstated in 2011. Because of the blacklist, his name had been stripped from the credits when the movie was released in 1953. Over time, many more people in the movie industry were blacklisted and denied work, some for the rest of their lives.

In response to the so-called "godless communists," studios churned out a series of popular biblical epics. Director Cecil B. DeMille, famous since the days of silent movies, started the trend in 1949 when he directed *Samson and Delilah*, a film based on characters from the Old Testament. In 1953, the first film in CinemaScope, or wide-screen, was *The Robe*, an epic starring Richard Burton playing a Roman military leader who commands the unit that crucifies Jesus. A giant hit, *The Robe* won a Golden Globe award for Best Motion Picture and spawned a sequel that came out a year later, *Demetrius and the Gladiators*.

Then in 1956, movie screens everywhere showed the most famous biblical epic of them all: *The Ten Commandments*, a retelling of the story of Moses leading the Jewish slaves out of Egypt and into the Promised Land. One of the great special effects of the day showed Moses, played by Charlton Heston, raising his arms to the heavens as the Red Sea parted, allowing the Jews to escape Egyptian soldiers. *The Ten Commandments* was the highest-grossing film in 1957, earning a net profit of $185 million, equal to nearly $1 billion today.

Charlton Heston returned to the screen in the decade's last biblical epic, *Ben-Hur* (1959). It told the story of Christ's final years through the eyes of an enslaved Jewish sympathizer who becomes a well-known chariot racer. The movie won a record-setting eleven Academy Awards. (This record would later be matched by *Titanic* in 1997 and *The Lord of the Rings: The Return of the King* in 2003.) The biblical movies of the 1950s were a clear token of their times. With many in the country feeling threatened by the cold war, American filmgoers flocked to movies that reaffirmed their religious beliefs and preached the gospel of freedom.

ANTICOMMUNIST FEATURE FILMS

With the fear of communism on the rise in the United States, the late 1940s and 1950s saw a stream of movies with blatantly anticommunist titles. Several of the most notable were *Behind the Iron Curtain* (1948), *I Married a Communist* (1949), *The Thing From Another World* (1951), *I Was a Communist for the FBI* (1951), *Atomic City* (1952), *Red Planet Mars* (1952), *Prisoner of War* (1954), and *Red Nightmare* (1957).

One of the most fondly remembered horror movies of the decade was *The Invasion of the Body Snatchers* (1956), a film in which the members of a small U.S. town are taken over by "body snatchers" who systematically strip each person of his or her unique characteristics, turning the town into a community of robot-like droids. Today, the story is seen as an expression of Americans' fear of communism, a system of belief that people worried would strip them of their individuality.

BIGGER IS BETTER

After the rationing of many nonessentials during World War II, Americans celebrated their new postwar prosperity by eagerly purchasing luxury items, such as homes, cars, and the newest invention of them all: television sets.

As TVs became more and more common, the movie industry did what it could to keep its audience—namely, entice viewers to movie theaters where the screens were larger and the sound was clearer than on television. In the 1950s and early 1960s, Hollywood introduced technology geared toward making movies bigger than ever. In 1953, 20th Century Fox introduced CinemaScope, a process of shooting a movie that allowed it to be shown on a larger screen. A year later, Paramount jumped on board, introducing VistaVision, a variant of the standard 35-mm film that allowed for shooting in wide-screen format. One of the first movies in 3-D was *Bwana Devil* (1952), an African adventure that promised audiences that lions would jump out of the screen.

For a while, these new techniques got the public away from their televisions and into theaters, but, eventually, the excitement wore thin. When the lure of movies made with new technology stopped attracting moviegoers, the formats were dropped. By that time, studio executives had learned that they would need to attract audiences the old-fashioned way: by telling entertaining and emotionally intense stories.

In an effort to maintain an audience Hollywood studios feared they were losing to TV, a stream of 3-D movies such as *Bwana Devil* was released—to what turned out to be less than enthusiastic crowds.

THE ANTIHERO

The 1950s are often idealized as a golden decade in American history, a time when families consisted of firm but fair fathers, conscientious mothers, and obedient children who rarely, if ever, got into trouble. This positive view of the 1950s has a grain of truth. It is based on the prosperity of the American middle class during the post-war years. Families moved to the suburbs in pursuit of the American dream. But underneath the image of the happy family, American youth were becoming restless, yearning for freedom and wanting to break the rules that controlled their lives. Though the youth revolt was still a decade away, movies of the 1950s portrayed unruly teenagers who saw life on very different terms from their parents.

James Dean starred in only three films before his tragic death at age twenty-four. Even so, his influence was enormous. Handsome and brooding, Dean became America's first teen idol with a dark side. His most influential role was in *Rebel Without a Cause* (1955). Playing Jim Stark, a troubled Los Angeles teenager who is new in town, Stark gets into a knife fight with a school rival and wins a famous game of "chicken," in which he and another boy drive toward a cliff and jump out at the last second before their cars crash. The movie ends with the police accidentally shooting one of Stark's friends. Sal Mineo and Natalie Wood costarred in the film. James Dean's role is notable because he played one of cinema's first teenage lost souls, a boy searching for answers, but not finding them.

Rebel Without a Cause wasn't the only movie of the decade to feature this new look at American youth. In 1953 *The Wild One* featured Marlon Brando as Johnny Strabler, the leader of a motorcycle gang that terrorizes the citizens of a small town. The movie is famous for one particular exchange. Strabler is asked by a local girl, "What are you rebelling against?" He

When James Dean starred in *Rebel Without A Cause* he became America's premier teenage bad-boy heartthrob. Sadly, he lived his legend in real life and died much too young in a car crash.

replies, "Whatdoyagot?" Today, the thugs of *The Wild One* may seem almost quaint. But at the time of its release, Brando and his gang of motorcyclists represented something very frightening—a teenage rebellion that went far beyond refusing to take out the trash or walk the dog. *Rebel Without a Cause* and *The Wild One* gave voice to an unease that would simmer for another decade before exploding in the 1960s.

A GRITTIER REALISM

Marlon Brando was well-known even before his appearance in *The Wild One.* He had starred in Tennessee Williams's Broadway play, *A Streetcar Named Desire*, which was made into a successful movie in 1951. Portraying blue-collar worker Stanley Kowalski with shocking realism, Brando was the first of a new kind of star: a method actor whose primary interest was in bringing out a character's inner turmoil with as much immediacy as possible. Brando was nominated for the Academy Award for Best Actor five times between 1951 and 1957.

The decade also gave rise to other talented young actors. Montgomery Clift began as a stage actor and soon became one of the decade's biggest movie stars, playing a series of complex heroes. In 1948, Clift starred in *The Search*, the story of a concentration camp survivor who searches for his mother in post–World War II Europe. Clift's work in the movie was thought to be so real that someone asked the film's director, Fred Zinnemann, "How did you find a soldier who acts so well?" Other famous roles in which Clift excelled included doomed soldier Robert E. Lee Prewitt in *From Here to Eternity* (1953) and bullied Jewish soldier Noah Ackerman in *The Young Lions* (1958). Movie audiences embraced actors like Clift, who seemed like real people, rather than the larger-than-life idols of the decades past.

As Brando, Clift, and other talented new actors emerged, movies themselves began to address the more difficult issues of the day. In 1950, Marlon Brando played a disabled World War II veteran in *The Men.* In 1954, Brando won an Academy Award for his portrayal of Terry Malloy in *On the Waterfront*, a film that boldly took on the subject of union violence among longshoremen in Hoboken, New Jersey. It was thought by many to be a response by director Elia Kazan to the Hollywood Ten's criticism of his having "named names" during the McCarthy era. The film's hero was a man who snitched against his own colleagues in favor of what was morally "right."

In 1958, a young Paul Newman impressed audiences with his truthful portrayal of an alcoholic former athlete in another Tennessee Williams adaptation, *Cat on a Hot Tin Roof*. Even

Movie stars of the 1950s seemed eager to break away from the glamour of the pre-war era. Paul Newman and Elizabeth Taylor turned heads as the unhappy couple at the heart of *Cat on a Hot Tin Roof*.

Frank Sinatra, the singer known best for appearing in light-hearted musical comedies, broke barriers by playing a heroin addict in 1955's *The Man with the Golden Arm*.

DECADE IN REVIEW

Of course, not every movie made in the 1950s featured weighty subjects such as heroin addiction. Many people went to the movies to have fun. The decade featured great slapstick comedy by Abbott and Costello as well as some of film's greatest westerns, such as John Ford's *The Searchers* (1956), starring John Wayne. The decade also produced some of the best musicals ever made. In 1952, Gene Kelly, Donald O'Connor, and Debbie Reynolds sang and danced their way through *Singin' in the Rain*, a brilliant spoof of Hollywood's reaction to the invention of "talkies." In 1953, Fred Astaire starred in one of his best films, *The Band Wagon*.

The list of great films goes on and on. Part of the fun of seeing a movie can be to escape from everyday problems and concerns. Though the 1950s introduced a new realism to cinema, the decade also produced a stream of movies with no greater goal than to give joy to an audience ready to be entertained.

The 1950s was not only about realism. *Singin' in the Rain* is a lighthearted look at the switch from silent movies to "talkies" that delights movie audiences to this day.

ACADEMY AWARD WINNERS FOR BEST PICTURE

So as to include all films that are released in a given year for award consideration, the Academy Awards ceremony is held the following year. For example, the awards for the 1950 films were given out in 1951.

1950: *All About Eve*
All About Eve is the story of an aging actress who befriends a younger, adoring fan, not realizing that the fan is plotting to manipulate her, replace her as a star, and seduce the man who loves her.

1951: *An American in Paris*
The musical *An American in Paris* starred Gene Kelly as an American World War II veteran and expatriate and Leslie Caron as a French waitress. The two fall in love even though she is engaged to another man. Her fiancé, upon overhearing the two saying good-night to each other at a masked ball, lets her out of the engagement.

1952: *The Greatest Show on Earth*
Set in the Ringling Bros. and Barnum & Bailey Circus, *The Greatest Show on Earth* centers around the general manager of the circus as he attempts to keep the show running in a postwar economy, while gangsters hustle the Midway, and the FBI investigates one of his employees.

1953: *From Here to Eternity*
Based on the book by James Jones, *From Here to Eternity* focuses on the lives of American soldiers stationed in Hawaii in the months leading up to the Japanese attack on Pearl Harbor, which led to the U.S. involvement in World War II.

1954: *On the Waterfront*
Based on the Pulitzer Prize–winning articles by Malcolm Johnson that ran in the New York *Sun*, *On the Waterfront* is the story of mob informers working on a union-controlled dock in Hoboken, New Jersey. The film follows the main character as he comes to the decision to testify against the mob-associated union leader.

1955: *Marty*
Marty tells the tale of a lonely man named Marty who, because he is so homely, has given up on the idea of love and marriage. But all that changes when he meets Clara.

1956: *Around the World in 80 Days*
Based on the Jules Verne novel, *Around the World in 80 Days* is about the adventures of a man who places a bet that he can circle the globe in a helium balloon and return to his social club in eighty days.

1957: *The Bridge on the River Kwai*
The Bridge on the River Kwai tells the dramatic story of American prisoners of war who were building a railroad-crossing bridge over the River Kwai in Thailand when they were captured by Japanese soldiers during World War II.

1958: *Gigi*
Based on the novella by French writer Colette, *Gigi* is the love story of the wealthy bachelor Gaston and his childhood friend, Gigi, who is training to become a courtesan.

1959: *Ben-Hur*
Ben-Hur is a biblical epic of the life of Jesus Christ, as told by Judah Ben-Hur, who goes from being a prince to a galley slave to a charioteer in Jerusalem.

1960s:

The World Unplugged

THE 1960s WAS A DECADE FRAUGHT WITH change. The country elected the young and handsome John F. Kennedy as president in 1960. A World War II veteran, Kennedy underscored American toughness, saying in his inaugural address, "Let every nation know . . . that we shall pay any price, bear any burden, meet any hardship, support any friend, oppose any foe, to assure the survival and the success of liberty." These were strong words. But by the end of the decade, the United States was far less sure of itself, despite a host of long overdue advancements in the nation's social fabric.

Martin Luther King Jr. led the civil rights movement to push for legislation ensuring equal rights. President Kennedy and, after Kennedy's assassination, President Lyndon Johnson worked to pass the landmark Civil Rights Act of 1964, a law that finally guaranteed African Americans basic rights long taken for granted by white males in the United States. At the urging of President Johnson, Congress passed Medicare and Medicaid laws that provided health insurance to the poor and to senior citizens.

But the nation also went to war in Vietnam with the stated

The 1960s became known as the decade of youth. Fittingly, it was ushered in by President John F. Kennedy who, at forty-three, was the youngest U.S. president ever elected, then or since.

objective of preventing it from falling prey to communism. The U.S. government feared that if Vietnam became communist, other Southeast Asian countries would, as well. As the war went on, however, thousands of young people were drafted into military service. It became clear that the United States was involved in an unwinnable civil war between North and South Vietnam. Protest movements sprang up throughout the United States. Champion boxer Muhammad Ali was stripped of his title and went to prison when he refused to fight in what he saw as an unjust war. Many men of draft age fled the country.

For those who remained, the youth movement exploded. All across the country young people took to the streets protesting the war. Equal rights protests began as well. Women marched for liberation, and black power movements took off. With the assassinations of President Kennedy in 1963, and Senator Robert Kennedy and Martin Luther King Jr. in 1968, what had begun as a movement for peaceful change became darker and, in some cases, more violent.

How did movies reflect the massive changes taking place in the country? While there was an array of successful family films—musicals, comedies, and westerns—many filmmakers responded to societal changes more directly. The end of the decade gave way to antiwar, antiestablishment films such as *Easy Rider*. A new wave of filmmakers in the 1960s brought more grittiness and realism to the screen than had previously been seen.

WAR IN THE 1960S

The 1960s began with a number of movies that were set in World War II, in which the United States and its armed forces were portrayed as heroes. Two of the best-received films were *The Great Escape* (1963), about an escape from a German prisoner of war camp, and *The Dirty Dozen* (1967), in which a U.S. Army major and a group of convicted GIs attempt to kill as many German leaders as possible. Despite the success of these two films, most other popular war movies of the decade mirrored the public's increasingly jaded view of both the military and the arms race with Russia.

In 1963, the world teetered briefly on the edge of a nuclear war when the United States discovered that the Soviet Union had a missile base in Cuba. The Cuban Missile Crisis ended

ROCK AND ROLL
AT THE MOVIES

Perhaps no other genre demonstrates the changing times of the 1960s more than movies conceived around the talent of famous rock stars. By 1960, Elvis Presley had already starred in four movies—all with largely predictable plots in which Elvis played a host of clean-cut characters. Throughout the 1960s, Elvis starred in hits such as *Blue Hawaii* (1961) and *Viva Las Vegas* (1964). But though Elvis remained popular, a new musical act called The Beatles had burst onto the scene. The group starred in *A Hard Day's Night* (1964), considered by many to be the best rock movie of all time. Essentially a day in the life of the Fab Four, *A Hard Day's Night* featured a hipper, more ironic sensibility that moviegoers found refreshing. Other Beatles films followed, including *Help!* (1965) and *Yellow Submarine* (1968), featuring the group's excellent music and tell-tale wit.

In 1969, the most popular rock stars of the day, including Jimi Hendrix, Joan Baez, James Taylor, the group Crosby, Stills and Nash, and many others, put on a three-day rock concert in Bethel, New York, attended by about 500,000 people. So many people tried to drive to the Woodstock Music Festival that the New York State Thruway had to be closed to traffic, meaning thousands couldn't get there and thousands more couldn't get anywhere. The resulting film, *Woodstock*, with a title song by Joni Mitchell, one of the many who couldn't get to the festival, depicted the countercultural youth movement in full swing.

without nuclear incident when the Soviet Union agreed to remove the missiles. However, Americans were terrified for the thirteen days before the Russians backed down. It had not been so long since an atomic bomb had been detonated in Hiroshima; with the cold war in full bloom, everyone believed a nuclear war could occur.

The assassination of President Kennedy on November 22, 1963, shocked the nation. In response to a scarier world, 1964 saw two ground-breaking war movies: *Dr. Strangelove or: How I Learned to Stop Worrying and Love the Bomb*, and *Fail-Safe*. Starring British comic actor Peter Sellers, *Dr. Strangelove* tells the tale of an unhinged U.S. general who orders a first-strike nuclear attack on Russia. A brilliant satire of the nuclear arms race, the movie ends with Slim Pickins's character whooping joyously as he rides an atomic bomb like a cowboy. *Fail Safe* tells the chilling tale of a military unable to stop a malfunctioning computer from triggering a nuclear crisis. Both films highlighted Americans' continuing fears of nuclear war.

FILMS GET RISQUÉ

In the 1950s, sex in Hollywood movies took place off-screen and only between married couples. But in 1960 things changed. Billy Wilder was one of the most talented people in the industry, writing and directing such classics as *Sunset Boulevard* (1950), *Stalag 17* (1953), and *Some Like It Hot* (1959). In 1960, Wilder directed *The Apartment*. Starring Jack Lemmon, the comedy was about a young, single accountant who lends out his small apartment to a rotating list of married executives in need of a place to bring their girlfriends.

Though tame by today's standards, *The Apartment* was one of the first movies to feature men cheating on their wives. Additionally, Wilder highlighted a darker side of the American dream. At a time when people's faith in public and private

THE RATINGS SYSTEM

In the late 1960s the motion picture industry adopted a new rating system introduced by the Motion Picture Association of America (MPAA). Starting in November 1968, each movie released in the United States was required to carry a rating, indicating its target audience and restricting certain viewers.

G: General audiences (all ages admitted).

M: Suggested for mature audiences. Parental discretion advised, but all ages admitted.

R: Restricted. Anyone under age seventeen not admitted unless accompanied by a parent or adult guardian.

X: Adults only. Anyone under age seventeen will not be admitted.

Studios quickly began to jockey for the ratings they thought would bring their films the largest audiences. *Midnight Cowboy* (1969), for example, was first released with an X rating. After trimming some risqué scenes, the film was rereleased as an R-rated film, allowing more customers to see it.

However, it quickly became apparent that the code had large problems. In 1970, the M rating was changed to GP, for "parental guidance suggested." Because the rating GP did not indicate the film's content, in 1972 explanations were added to the rating. Statements such as, "Contains material not generally suitable for pre-teenagers" told parents why the film received its rating. Additionally, the MPAA changed the acronym of GP rating to PG.

In 1984, *Indiana Jones and the Temple of Doom* was released with a PG rating. Many parents who had taken their children to see the film became outraged because it contained so much violence and gore, which they had no knowledge of before seeing the film. Steven Spielberg, the director of the *Indiana Jones* films, suggested that the MPAA create a new rating for films that were too adult for PG, but not adult enough for R. This led to the implementation of the PG-13 rating, which alerts parents that the content in the film may be too strong for children under age thirteen.

By the late 1980s, the X rating had become controversial. Although it indicated a non-pornographic adult film when the ratings system was created, many pornography studios began labeling their films as X-rated. Eventually an X-rated film became synonymous with pornography, so in 1989 the MPAA changed the X rating to an NC-17 rating, which alerted people that the film contained material that was not suitable for anyone under seventeen years old, but was not a pornographic film.

Now the rating system is as follows:

G: General Audiences—All Ages Admitted
PG: Parental Guidance Suggested—Some Material May Not be Suitable for Children
PG-13: Parents Strongly Cautioned—Some Material May Be Inappropriate for Children Under 13
R: Restricted: Under 17 Requires Accompanying Parent or Adult Guardian
NC-17: No One 17 and Under Admitted

Additionally, the film's rating and the reasons for it are shown on-screen before the film runs. Reasons for adult ratings typically include language, sexual content, and alcohol and drug use.

institutions would be brought into question, *The Apartment* features a hero whose hopes of getting ahead have nothing to do with merit and hard work and everything to do with helping his bosses cheat on their wives. A great success, *The Apartment* won the Academy Award for Best Picture in 1960 and is shown on TV to this day.

Another movie that highlighted a growing openness about sex was 1961's *Breakfast at Tiffany's*. Based on a Truman Capote novella, the movie starred Audrey Hepburn as a single woman living in New York. Again, tame by today's standards, *Breakfast at Tiffany's* was one of the first movies to feature unmarried characters who were understood to be having sex as a matter of course.

Another film to take a looser view of sex was the massively popular *Tom Jones* (1963), based on the famous 1749 novel by Henry Fielding. Sexually suggestive and bawdy, *Tom Jones* starred Albert Finney as a British rogue who, banished from his home, goes on a rollicking adventure that leads him from bed to bed.

The tail end of the decade brought Paul Mazursky's *Bob & Carol & Ted & Alice* (1969) to U.S. screens. The film opens with Bob and Carol, played by Robert Culp and Natalie Wood, deciding to open their marriage so that they can have sex with whomever they want. Ultimately, Bob and Carol end up in Las Vegas, attempting a foursome with their married friends Ted and Alice. The couples are actually depicted in bed, if still not engaging in sex. A huge hit, Mazursky's film led to a stream of other movies featuring infidelity and wife swapping.

Other movies of the 1960s dramatized the darker side of relationships. In 1966, Elizabeth Taylor and Richard Burton starred in Edward Albee's *Who's Afraid of Virginia Woolf?*, a scathing look at a long-decayed marriage. The following year, *The Graduate* was released. In the film, Dustin Hoffman plays Benjamin Braddock, an aimless college graduate who is seduced by Mrs. Robinson, the wife of his father's business partner. The plot thickens when Benjamin falls in love with Mrs. Robinson's daughter, Elaine. In the end, Benjamin and Elaine escape together from the church in which she is getting married to another, more conventional, man. But it is not a traditional happy ending. Benjamin and Elaine ride silently into the sunset on a public bus to the strains of Simon and Garfunkel's melancholy "The Sounds of Silence," a song about the difficulty people have in forging meaningful connections.

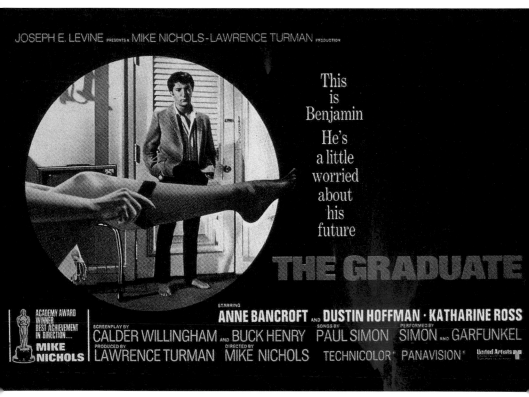

The 1960s was a groundbreaking time in culture and cinema. *The Graduate*, **about a lost young man who sleeps with a friend of his mother's and then falls for her daughter, broke many taboos, not least among them destroying the myth of the contented suburban housewife.**

In an era when Americans had grown disillusioned with their government, they were also increasingly skeptical about the possibility of love bringing lifelong happiness.

REBELS WITH A CAUSE

At the end of the 1960s, the streets exploded in protest at the Vietnam War and anger at those in power, known as the "Establishment." A generation of young people were rebelling against a government they felt they could not trust. Some landmark films of the 1960s reflected the change in mood. In 1967, *Bonnie and Clyde* became a surprise hit. The fictionalized tale of the notorious bank-robbing team stood out for its realistic violence and sexually frank situations. *Easy Rider*, a low-budget film released in 1969, depicted countercultural motorcyclists traveling from Los Angeles to New Orleans in search of America. In a surprise ending, highlighting the stark divisions in the country, the bikers are shot by a trucker and left for dead. Made without the backing of a major Hollywood studio, *Easy Rider* is also credited with launching the independent film industry.

The same year, the winner of the Academy Award for Best Picture was *Midnight Cowboy*, another movie that dramatized life on the fringes of society. The story concerns Joe Buck (played by Jon Voight), a young Texan who comes to New York to work as a male prostitute. Soon Buck meets down-and-out, sickly Ratso Rizzo (played by Dustin Hoffman). The two form an odd friendship, trying to survive the hardships of life in New York City. Eventually, they leave New York, traveling south by bus. The movie ends with Ratso's death. It is hard to imagine a movie that highlights the darker undertones of a decade more clearly.

Easy Rider followed the wave of the 1950s rebel movies. A decade later, though, the 1960s rebels were fueled by drugs, sex, and disillusionment.

PANDO COMPANY en association avec RAYBERT PRODUCTIONS
présente

easy rider

PETER FONDA · DENNIS HOPPER JACK NICHOLSON

Scénario écrit par PETER FONDA   Produit par PETER FONDA   Réalisé par DENNIS HOPPER
DENNIS HOPPER   Producteur associé WILLIAM HAYWARD
TERRY SOUTHERN   Producteur délégué BERT SCHNEIDER

Distribué par WARNER COLUMBIA FILM

TWO WESTERNS

Hollywood also released two popular, though ironic, westerns in 1969. *True Grit* told the tale of a U.S. Marshal setting out to catch a murderer, but only at the behest of the fourteen-year-old daughter of the victim. The movie earned John Wayne an Oscar for Best Actor for playing against type as a drunken antihero who, nevertheless, shows "true grit." The second was *Butch Cassidy and the Sundance Kid*, a fictional retelling of the lives of the famed train and bank robbers. An immensely entertaining movie, *Butch Cassidy* is a feel-good film with a twist. Laced with contemporary, ironic dialogue, the film does not have a traditional happy ending though its heroes are comedic and sympathetic, unlike traditional movie outlaws.

DECADE IN REVIEW

As with all eras since the dawn of cinema, the 1960s had its share of upbeat movies. In fact, three of the biggest hits of the decade were musicals: *My Fair Lady* (1964), *Mary Poppins* (1964), and *The Sound of Music* (1965). *Funny Girl* (1968) and *Hello, Dolly!* (1969) were also successful movie musicals. The 1960s also saw a wave of highly silly movies in keeping with the irreverent spirit of the Beatles' *A Hard Day's Night*. The most notable was 1963's *It's a Mad, Mad, Mad, Mad World*, a star-studded epic in which the dying words of a thief spark a world-wide treasure hunt.

In 1968 Mel Brooks made his first film, *The Producers*, a satire about a Broadway producer who decides to create a Broadway show called *Springtime for Hitler* because he is sure

Bonnie and Clyde **glorified crime and criminals, in keeping with the "what's out is in" ethos of the post-Beatles 1960s.**

it will flop. Instead, the play is a giant success. It has become a cult classic and inspired a prize-winning, hit Broadway show, as well.

Two 1967 films, both starring Sidney Poitier, had huge impacts that year. In *To Sir, with Love*, Poitier played Mark Thackeray, who, because he can't get a job as an engineer, the career for which he had trained, takes a job teaching school in a working-class neighborhood in London's East End. Like so many other inspirational movies about teachers, *To Sir, with Love* was something of a sentimental tearjerker. What made it different was that Poitier's skin color was treated almost incidentally. In a risqué fashion for the time, Lulu, one of the white students, develops a crush on him. Soon thousands of young girls of every race or ethnicity who saw the rising young star in this movie would feel the same way.

Poitier also starred in Norman Jewison's *In the Heat of the Night* (1967). Based on the novel by John Ball, the film tells the story of Virgil Tibbs, a respected African American detective from Philadelphia. Tibbs, a homicide expert, is sent to Mississippi to solve the murder of a wealthy Chicago land developer who had planned to build a factory in the fictional town of Sparta, Mississippi. The film displayed the animosity between white Southerners and black Northerners, and it showed that the only way to change such deep-seated attitudes was by working together and earning one another's respect. A classic exchange in the film is when Rod Steiger's character asks Poitier, "What do they call you up there [in Philadelphia]?" and Poitier responds, "They call me Mr. Tibbs."

Among the barriers broken by the 1960s' cinema was the introduction of blacks as leading men. Sidney Poitier broke the barrier in such well-received films as *To Sir With Love*, *Guess Who's Coming to Dinner*, and (*pictured here*) the award-winning *In the Heat of the Night*.

In another famous scene, Tibbs is slapped by a wealthy white man whom he is interrogating. In the original screenplay, Tibbs does not react to the slap, but Poitier requested that the scene be changed so that Tibbs reacts by slapping the white man back.

It was one of the first films to depict an African American reacting in such a way, and it sent shockwaves through the nation. Despite the passage of the Civil Rights Act of 1964, the nation was still deeply divided on racial issues. *In the Heat of the Night* went on to receive five Academy Awards, including Best Picture.

The tenor of any time period is best measured by the movies that pushed social boundaries the furthest. By that measure, dark, character-driven movies such as *The Graduate* and *Midnight Cowboy* pointed the way toward the future and one of film's most creatively exciting periods: the early 1970s.

ACADEMY AWARD WINNERS OF BEST PICTURE

So as to include all films that are released in a given year for award consideration, the Academy Awards ceremony is held the following year. For example, the awards for the 1960 films were given out in 1961.

1960: *The Apartment*

The story of an ambitious employee who allows his bosses to use his apartment to conduct their extramarital affairs, *The Apartment* was one of the first films to depict unapologetic adultery on screen.

1961: *West Side Story*

Featuring music by Leonard Bernstein, lyrics by Stephen Sondheim, and choreography by Jerome Robbins, *West Side Story* is a musical based on Shakespeare's *Romeo and Juliet*, but cast as a fight between two rival gangs in 1950s New York City.

1962: *Lawrence of Arabia*

Considered by many to be one of the greatest and most influential films ever made, *Lawrence of Arabia* tells the story of British army lieutenant T. E. Lawrence and his time in Arabia during World War I. The film shows Lawrence's emotional struggles in coping with the violence of war and his ethical dilemma regarding his divided loyalty to his country and his Arabian friends.

1963: *Tom Jones*

Based on the 1749 novel *The History of Tom Jones, a Foundling,* by Henry Fielding, the film tells the story of the title character, an illegitimate child raised by a wealthy man. Jones is sent away to make his fortune because of his seemingly dissolute life.

1964: *My Fair Lady*

The film adaptation of the Broadway musical, which itself was based upon George Bernard Shaw's play *Pygmalion*, *My Fair Lady* is the story of Henry Higgins, an arrogant phonetics professor who accepts a bet that he can teach any woman to speak well enough to be presented as a duchess at a high-society ball.

1965: *The Sound of Music*

The Sound of Music, set in pre–World War II Austria, is based on the true story of the singing von Trapp family and their governess.

1966: *A Man for All Seasons*

A Man for All Seasons is the cinematic biography of Sir Thomas More, the Lord Chancellor of England, who was beheaded when he refused to sign a letter asking the Pope for permission to grant King Henry VIII a divorce.

1967: *In the Heat of the Night*

Based on the novel by John Ball, *In the Heat of the Night* is a murder mystery set in racist, rural Mississippi. African American detective Virgil Tibbs is sent from Philadelphia to assist a white, bigoted local police chief on the case.

1968: *Oliver!*

Oliver!, the musical adaptation of Charles Dickens's novel *Oliver Twist*, is the story of an orphan who falls in with Fagin, a criminal who commands a team of young orphans and trains them to be pickpockets.

1969: *Midnight Cowboy*

Midnight Cowboy, based on the novel by James Leo Herlihy, is about two men, Joe Buck and Ratso Rizzo, who make their meager living by conning, hustling, and hooking in New York City.

THREE

1970s:
From Despair to the Blockbuster

REPUBLICAN RICHARD M. NIXON WON THE
presidency in 1968, with the promise of bringing "peace with
honor" to Vietnam. Upon taking office in January 1969, however, he increased the number of troops sent to war. Then, in
the early 1970s, Nixon ordered U.S. planes to bomb neighboring Cambodia, enraging those Americans who were already
fiercely opposed to the war.

Even so, Nixon's first term had some marked successes. In
1970, Nixon formed the Environmental Protection Agency to
oversee the implementation of the Clean Air and Clean Water
Acts, a set of laws to help decrease air and water pollution.
In 1972, Nixon became the first American president to visit
Communist China. He also signed historic arms control agreements with the Soviet Union.

But shortly after, Nixon's presidency began to unravel.
After winning reelection by a landslide in 1972, Republican
Party employees went on trial for having broken into Dem-
ocratic National Headquarters at the Watergate Hotel in
Washington, D.C. during the election. The resulting cover-up
of the crime, which involved President Nixon as an "unindicted

The 1970s were a tumultuous decade, with much of the nation torn by cultural and political conflicts over issues including women's rights, the Vietnam War, and even how to make a living. One of the bright spots was President Richard Nixon's trip to Communist China, which opened trade between the two nations.

coconspirator," is now known as the Watergate scandal. It led Nixon to resign in August 1974 rather than face impeachment.

In 1976, Georgia governor Jimmy Carter, a Democrat, was elected president, promising to bring the country together. However, Carter, a Washington outsider, had trouble passing his ambitious programs through Congress. Though Carter brokered a watershed peace agreement between Israel and Egypt in 1978, his presidency also saw the revolutionary government in Iran take fifty-two Americans hostage. The subsequent oil crisis led to gas shortages at home, causing gas prices to skyrocket.

Many believe that great pain can lead to great art. So it was that the tumultuous events of the 1970s helped feed one of the great decades of American film. A new wave of actors, directors, and screenwriters produced a stream of excellent films that questioned American institutions. By the end of the decade, a new phenomenon had occurred in American movies: the blockbuster. The huge successes of *Jaws* in 1975 and *Star Wars* in 1977 changed the movie business and moviegoing forever.

QUESTIONING AUTHORITY

Hollywood responded to the Vietnam War and the Watergate scandal with a series of films that took a critical look at the U.S. government and its institutions. Perhaps the most subversive movie of the decade was *M*A*S*H* (1970), a wickedly funny look at life in a mobile medical unit in the Korean War of the early 1950s. The use of the Korean War as a background was a clear allusion to the war in Vietnam. Donald Sutherland and Elliot Gould played Hawkeye Pierce and Trapper John, leaders of a highly irreverent group of doctors who, between surgeries, drank, played infantile practical jokes, and stole Jeeps. This was the antithesis of the thought and sentiment surrounding World War II, the so-called "good war."

U.S. participation in Vietnam ended in 1973. In 1975, Saigon, the capital of South Vietnam, fell to the North Vietnamese, and the Vietnam War ended. After more than ten years of U.S. involvement, Hollywood finally began to address the war's horrors more directly. By the end of the 1970s, three cutting-edge films had given voice to conflicts felt by Americans during the war. In 1978, Jane Fonda, Jon Voight, and Bruce Dern starred in *Coming Home*, the story of a married woman who falls in love with a paralyzed Vietnam veteran while her husband is serving in Vietnam. The movie showed the traumatic physical and psychological effects of the war. The same year, *The Deer Hunter* explored Vietnam's chilling effects on a group of friends from a blue-collar town in Pennsylvania. Francis Ford Coppola's epic *Apocalypse Now*, a surreal and horrifying look at the war, loosely based on Joseph Conrad's novel *Heart of Darkness*, came to theaters in 1979. One of the film's more memorable scenes shows a soldier, played by Robert Duvall, looking over the devastating scene of a napalm-bombed beach, brightly saying, "I love the smell of napalm in the morning."

HOLLYWOOD SEES THE FUTURE

Usually, art imitates life. Sometimes, though, it seems as if life imitates art. Late in March of 1979 there was a dangerous accident at Three Mile Island, a nuclear power plant in Harrisburg, Pennsylvania. *The China Syndrome* had premiered just two weeks earlier. In the film, a reporter discovers a cover-up of safety hazards at a nuclear power plant.

Based on Joseph Conrad's early twentieth-century novel, *Heart of Darkness*, Francis Ford Coppola's *Apocalypse Now* showed a darkness at the heart of war that had not previously been seen in movies.

43

ACTORS REFLECT A TOUGHER TIME

In the 1970s, a new generation of Hollywood directors and actors was off and running, producing movies that took on a host of difficult subjects. In 1972, Jane Fonda won the Academy Award for Best Actress for her role as a classy, intelligent prostitute in *Klute* (1971). The same year, Gene Hackman won Best Actor for playing "Popeye" Doyle, a New York City narcotics cop, in *The French Connection*. In 1972, heart-throb Burt Reynolds starred in *Deliverance*, a grisly tale of a violent camping trip. In 1972 and 1974, *The Godfather* and *The Godfather: Part II* starred Marlon Brando and Al Pacino as patriarchs of the fictional Corleone Mafia family. Each of these movies mirrored the cynicism of the times by depicting people who lived in corrupt environments, outside the realm of conventional society.

In 1973, Al Pacino starred in *Serpico*. It was based on the true story of a New York City policeman named Frank Serpico, who was shot after refusing to take bribes. In 1974, Dustin Hoffman starred in *Lenny*, about ground breaking 1950s comedian Lenny Bruce. Bruce had died of a heroin overdose in 1966, ending a brilliant career that laid the basis for modern comedy, from *Saturday Night Live* to Richard Pryor to Chris Rock.

In 1975, Jack Nicholson played Randle McMurphy in the film adaptation of Ken Kesey's novel *One Flew Over the Cuckoo's Nest*. Serving a short sentence for statutory rape, McMurphy is transferred to a mental hospital for evaluation. There, he runs afoul of the evil Nurse Ratched when he organizes his fellow patients against the hospital staff. Eventually, he is given a lobotomy to shut him up. The film questions who is sane and who is crazy.

The next year Robert DeNiro starred in *Taxi Driver* as a mentally unstable war veteran who drives a taxi and becomes obsessed with a young prostitute played by Jodie Foster. The film features a classic scene in which DeNiro's character looks at himself in the mirror and asks, "You talkin' to me?"

What do all of these movies have in common? Each one stars a talented actor who is willing to throw himself or herself headfirst into an unconventional leading role. Each movie tackles difficult subject matter, exposing the underbelly of American society. Not only are these some of the best-remembered films of the era, but they were also hits—movies that people saw and talked about.

THE DECADE'S BIGGEST STAR: ROBERT REDFORD

The leading movie star of the early 1970s was Robert Redford, who played the Sundance Kid in 1969's *Butch Cassidy and the Sundance Kid*. In keeping with the spirit of the times, Redford was not satisfied to star in light entertainment that would capitalize on his good looks. In *Downhill Racer* (1969) he played Dave Chapplett, an arrogant, unlikable skier who learns some tough lessons about what it means to win. In 1972, Redford played Bill McKay in *The Candidate*, which spoofed and questioned the U.S. government and elections. *Three Days of the Condor* (1975) was an engrossing thriller in which Redford played a CIA operative on the run from the U.S. government. Finally, Redford produced and costarred with Dustin Hoffman in *All the President's Men* (1976), a movie that tracked journalists Bob Woodward and Carl Bernstein's uncovering of the Watergate scandal. At the time, Redford didn't expect the film to be a hit, but the public mood was more serious than he had anticipated.

The success of such serious films is a testament to American moviegoers, who were interested in being provoked as well as entertained.

Richard Nixon's presidency was brought down by the cover-up of the burglary of the Democratic National Committee headquarters at the Watergate complex in Washington, D.C. Robert Redford, the leading star of the decade, costarred in *All the President's Men*, which told the story of the downfall of the Nixon administration.

A ROMANTIC THROWBACK

Dark times bring nostalgia. In 1970, *Love Story* became a smash hit. The movie told the tale of Oliver Barrett IV, a wealthy Harvard University student, and Jennifer Cavialleri, a working-class girl at neighboring Radcliffe College. The couple overcome class differences to fall in love and get married. *Love Story* spawned one of the best-known catchphrases in movie history, "Love means never having to say you're sorry." Its popularity also indicated that there was a sizable segment of the American public that wanted stories in which the young characters were neither protesting the war nor taking drugs.

A NEW LOOK AT RELATIONSHIPS

The 1970s is sometimes called "the Me decade," a time when people's focus turned to exploring their own feelings. As a result, TV was filled with shows in which the characters talked more openly about their insecurities and fears. Movies were no different. One of the most successful and original voices of the decade belonged to Woody Allen, a stand-up comedian from New York whose early films feature a fresh, neurotic wit. *Sleeper* (1973) is about a New York City man who wakes up over two hundred years in the future and ends up having to clone a fallen leader by using the leader's only remaining body part: his nose. *Love and Death* (1975) is a spoof set in czarist Russia.

In 1977, Allen broke new ground when he cowrote, directed, and starred in *Annie Hall*, a film that traced the history of the relationship between Alvy Singer, played by Allen, and Annie Hall, played by Diane Keaton. Told in a series of flashbacks, the movie paints one of the most complete pictures of a relationship in film history. In keeping with the open spirit of the times, Allen's characters are humorously upfront about love, sex,

In tune with the tenor of the times, *Annie Hall* is a love story that doesn't have a happy ending. What it does have, though, is plenty of humor and realism about romantic relationships.

and death. The movie does not end with Alvy Singer and Annie Hall walking happily into the sunset. Instead, the couple have parted ways. After watching the two share a friendly meal, the movie concludes with a voice-over by Allen:

> It was great seeing Annie again. I . . . I realized what a terrific person she was, and . . . and how much fun it was just knowing her; and I . . . I, I thought of that old joke, y'know, the, this . . . this guy goes to a psychiatrist and says, "Doc, uh, my brother's crazy; he thinks he's a chicken." And, uh, the doctor says, "Well, why don't you turn him in?" The guy says, "I would, but I need the eggs." Well, I guess that's pretty much now how I feel about relationships; y'know, they're totally irrational, and crazy, and absurd, and . . . but, uh, I guess we keep goin' through it because, uh, most of us . . . need the eggs.

The movie ends with an awareness of life's imperfections—mirroring an imperfect era.

CATCH THE FEVER

Based on a *New York* magazine article about a group of kids in Brooklyn who went dancing every Saturday night, *Saturday Night Fever* (1977) became one of the biggest movies of the decade. Featuring a set of songs by the Bee Gees, the movie turned John Travolta into a star and disco into a craze.

THE BLOCKBUSTERS

In 1975, Stephen Spielberg, a young, largely untested director, directed the film adaptation of a popular novel about a shark that wreaks havoc on a beach town on Cape Cod, Massachusetts. The resulting film, *Jaws*, made Spielberg a household name. Though an exciting, well-done tale, the significance of *Jaws* was more in its marketing than its content. Until the mid–1970s most movies were first released in a few theaters in major cities and then gradually introduced to the rest of the country. Due to *Jaws*' success in advance screenings, Universal Pictures decided to release the picture in hundreds of theaters across the country at the same time, on the same weekend. The gamble paid off brilliantly as *Jaws* became the movie event of the summer.

Jaws, the story of a shark that terrorizes a beach town, was both a blockbuster hit and the making of director Steven Spielberg.

Two summers later, another film by another young film-maker was released to similar success. Written, produced, and directed by George Lucas, *Star Wars* has permeated American culture, perhaps more than any other film. Featuring innovative special effects, *Star Wars* introduced the world to a host of beloved characters: Luke Skywalker, Princess Leia, Han Solo, Obi-Wan Kenobi, and Darth Vader.

Catchphrases from the film, most notably "May the force be with you," have become part of popular language. In the 1980s, Ronald Reagan's proposed missile defense program was nicknamed "Star Wars."

With the success of *Jaws* and *Star Wars*, Hollywood studios began to make movies with more of an eye toward how much money they would make during their opening weekend rather than in their overall run. As a result, executives began to look for sure-fire products: movies based on superheroes, famous books, or adaptations of TV shows—any subject that would immediately capture the public's imagination. As a result, quirky films and those with difficult subject matter were less likely to get made by big studios—a trend that continues to this day.

THE DECADE IN REVIEW

The 1970s remain one of the best decades in American movie-making. Spurred by audiences ready to see complex stories that featured morally compromised characters, a stream of talented young stars and directors rose brilliantly to the challenge. While *Jaws* and *Star Wars* might have started a new trend in movie marketing, the success of both films shows that the public will always flock to a well-told story.

Blaxploitation films, a controversial new genre that appealed to African Americans, came to cinemas in the 1970s. *Blaxploitation* is a blend of the words *black* and *exploitation*.

Exploitation films capitalize on sensationalistic content such as sex or violence. Blaxploitation films often revolved around crime, drug lords, and gangsters, featured white characters as antagonists, were set in ghettos, and featured soundtracks of funk, soul, and jazz music. The most famous of these films are *Sweet Sweetback's Baadasssss Song* (1971), *Shaft* (1971), and *Foxy Brown* (1974). Not all blaxploitation films were crime dramas. The blaxploitation genre grew to include horror films, musicals, and courtroom dramas, as well as the crime-centric films that began the trend.

Though these films were heralded by some as symbols of black empowerment, many saw them as perpetuating ignorant stereotypes. In an effort to end the genre, the National Association for the Advancement of Colored People (NAACP), the Southern Christian Leadership Conference, and the National Urban League created the Coalition Against Blaxploitation. Many African Americans working in the entertainment industry joined the movement, and by the late 1970s blaxploitation films were out of vogue.

It is perhaps also true that as the decade drew to a close, American audiences were growing tired of disillusionment and emotionally charged story-telling. *Jaws* and *Star Wars* were fun, clever films that anyone could enjoy. But as the decade ended, the mood of the country became more patriotic and less questioning. Hollywood focused on providing Americans with simpler entertainment.

ACADEMY AWARD WINNERS OF BEST PICTURE

So as to include all films that are released in a given year for award consideration, the Academy Awards ceremony is held the following year. For example, the awards for the 1970 films were given out in 1971.

1970: *Patton*
Patton is a biographical film about the decorated World War II U.S. general George Patton.

1971: *The French Connection*
An adaptation of the book by Robin Moore, *The French Connection* is a real-life drama about two New York City narcotics detectives who track the smuggling of heroin between Marseilles, France, and New York City.

1972: *The Godfather*
Based upon the novel by Mario Puzo, *The Godfather* chronicles a violent mob war that breaks out between the five families of the Italian Mafia in New York.

1973: *The Sting*
Starring Robert Redford and Paul Newman, *The Sting* is a crime comedy about two grifters who con a mob boss. It was, in its way, a sequel to *Butch Cassidy and the Sundance Kid*.

1974: *The Godfather: Part II*
The Godfather: Part II tells the story of the rise to power of Mafia boss Vito Corleone, who is an old man in the first movie. It continues the story of the Corleone family where the first film left off.

1975: *One Flew Over the Cuckoo's Nest*
One Flew Over the Cuckoo's Nest, based on the novel by Ken Kesey, tells the story of how McMurphy, played by Jack

Nicholson, befriends and becomes an advocate for the other mental patients on his hospital ward.

1976: *Rocky*

Written by and starring Sylvester Stallone, *Rocky* is the rags-to-riches story of a debt collector turned club boxer who gets a shot at winning the world heavyweight championship. The film was made on a budget of $1 million and was shot in just twenty-eight days.

1977: *Annie Hall*

Cowritten, directed by, and starring Woody Allen, the autobiographical *Annie Hall* follows the years-long relationship of Alvy Singer and Annie Hall (played by Woody Allen and Diane Keaton), told by Singer in flashbacks and by mock interviews with happily married senior citizens.

1978: *The Deer Hunter*

The Deer Hunter is about three friends from the same hometown who fight in the Vietnam War and are captured by the North Vietnamese. It became famous for several suspense-filled scenes and for depicting the horrors soldiers suffer both during and after returning from war.

1979: *Kramer vs. Kramer*

The story of an intense custody battle that ensues when Mrs. Kramer leaves her husband and child and then decides she wants custody of her young son. *Kramer vs. Kramer*, based on the novel by Avery Corman, showed the wrenching turmoil of the choices a woman in the 1970s made between life, love, and career.

FOUR

1980s:
The Reagan Years

ON JANUARY 20, 1980, RONALD REAGAN became the fortieth president of the United States. A former movie star, Reagan used his successful tenure as governor of California to become president. After the years of Vietnam, Watergate, and economic turmoil, Reagan's conservative outlook and disarming optimism reassured the American public that good times were still ahead. If the prevailing attitude of the 1960s was about using the government to help the poor, the 1980s looked to loosen the reins of government constraints so businesses could boom. After a major recession in the early part of the decade, a mergers-and-acquisitions rage took over the country. The 1980s became a time when the rich got richer and the poor got poorer. As investment banks outbid each other for companies, a love affair with wealth took over the country, and this attitude was reflected in many movies.

Along with a newfound economic muscle, Americans regained their confidence in the United States as a world superpower. After spending much of his early political career bashing communists, President Reagan signed a series of landmark disarmament agreements with Russia. As the Soviet system

When former actor Ronald Reagan became president in 1981, the worlds of Hollywood and Washington met in one man.

began to collapse in the late 1980s, Americans were pleased to discover that the cold war was over and that the United States was suddenly the world's only superpower.

BLOCKBUSTER MENTALITY

An American public that wanted to clear its collective mind after the complications of the 1960s and 1970s became attracted to different kinds of movies. In general, the serious, edgy films of the 1970s were brushed aside in favor of films made with an eye toward mass appeal. Following the blockbuster trend set by *Jaws* and *Star Wars*, the 1980s saw the introduction of the "high concept" film, a movie with a plot that could be explained in a few sentences. More and more, producers looked for movies that could be described as offshoots of previous hits. For instance, the 1979 hit *Alien* was famously described as "*Jaws* in space."

Talented directors, including superstars like Peter Bog-danovich, whose *The Last Picture Show* was a huge hit in 1971, fell upon hard times as studio executives focused on finding big event films that were more splashy than cerebral. These films generally relied on expensive special effects, were released during the summer, and featured at least one established movie star.

Of course, some blockbusters are excellent films. Though the 1980s didn't see many films like *Taxi Driver* or *Dog Day Afternoon*, the decade did produce many well-done, beloved movies. Leading the pack were Hollywood's new darling directors, George Lucas and Steven Spielberg. In the early 1980s, Lucas's *Star Wars* saga continued with *The Empire Strikes Back* (1980) and *Return of the Jedi* (1983). In 1981, the pair teamed up, with Lucas developing the story and Spielberg directing, to bring Indiana Jones to the screen in *Raiders of the Lost Ark*, a swashbuckling throwback to 1940s adventure films with modern special effects.

A man who defeats Nazi Germany using only a rope and

In movies such as _Raiders of the Lost Ark_, the 1980s ushered in what has now become an expected universe of massive special effects.

his wits, Indiana Jones, as played by Harrison Ford, was the perfect hero for a decade in which America was gearing up for a showdown with the so-called "evil empire" of the Soviet Union. _Star Wars_ and _Indiana Jones_ also helped spur the trend of sequels. There have now been four _Indiana Jones_ films and six _Star Wars_ movies. It seemed that moviegoers wanted to see familiar stories that they knew they would enjoy before they paid for their tickets.

Other movies made on a more modest scale also became huge hits. These included *Romancing the Stone* (1984) and *Back to the Future* (1985). In *Romancing the Stone*, a writer played by Kathleen Turner travels to Colombia to rescue her kidnapped sister, only to find herself in the thick of a dangerous adventure. The *Back to the Future* series wooed audiences with its first film, in which a high school boy played by Michael J. Fox travels thirty years back in time and meets his parents as teenagers. Horror films like *Halloween* (1978) and *Friday the 13th* (1980) were also massively successful franchises, each with many sequels.

Even though the predominant tenor of the 1980s film making wasn't about raising social issues, a powerful new director, Spike Lee, had great success with his funny, occasionally bitter, looks at race relations. Many moviegoers consider Lee's *Do the Right Thing* (1989)—a film that explores the tricky and sometimes inflammatory relationships between people of different races and ethnicities—to be one of the best movies of the decade.

Though Lee ushered in a new kind of urban filmmaking, other films of the 1980s also tackled race relations in the United States. In 1985 *The Color Purple* was a huge hit. Adapted from Alice Walker's novel, it depicted life for single black women in rural Georgia during the 1930s. The film was directed by Steven Spielberg and boasted a star cast including Whoopi Goldberg, Danny Glover, Oprah Winfrey, and Laurence Fishburne. The film was an enormous success both critically and at the box office, and it received eleven Academy Award nominations.

Another much-lauded film of the decade was *Driving Miss Daisy* (1989), based on the off-Broadway play by Alfred Uhry. The plot spans nearly thirty years and depicts the friendship between Daisy Werthan (played by Jessica Tandy), a Jewish widow living in Atlanta, and Hoke Colburn (played by Morgan Freeman), an African American man hired by Daisy's son to chauffeur her. The story also tackles the topic of prejudice

In a decade full of feel-good adventure stories, *Do the Right Thing* by young, black director Spike Lee stood out for its intelligence, edginess, and humor.

against Jews and African Americans. *Driving Miss Daisy* was nominated for nine Academy Awards, and won four, including Best Picture. In October 2010, it was given new life as a Broadway play starring Vanessa Redgrave (who was nominated for a Tony Award for her portrayal of Daisy) and James Earl Jones as Hoke.

THE COMING OF VIDEO

Today, movies are available practically everywhere: at theaters, on TV, through Netflix, Hulu, iTunes, and many other sources. But in the mid–1970s a moviegoer had one choice: the theater. And once a particular movie left the theaters, moviegoers couldn't see it again unless it was shown at a second-run theater or on television, often years later. That changed in the early 1980s. The widespread introduction of videocassette players, or VCRs, allowed audiences to watch their favorite films in the comfort of their own homes as many times as they liked. Viewers also soon had the option of renting videocassettes for limited time periods from a wave of video stores that seemed to open all at once, as well as from most public libraries. To Hollywood's relief, people still came to theaters for the big-screen, surround-sound experience that was not yet possible at home. But now, with more opportunities to see an important movie again and again, film had an even greater role in the culture.

A NEW LOOK AT VIETNAM

Oliver Stone has forged a reputation as a filmmaker who thrives on tackling important social issues. In the late 1980s he produced and directed two films that took the closest look at the war in Vietnam since *The Deer Hunter* in 1978. Notable for its harsh take on relations between American and North Vietnamese troops and its realistic battle scenes in the jungles of North Vietnam, *Platoon* (1986) was heralded as one of the sharpest looks at a painful chapter in America's past. Two years later, in 1989, Stone released *Born on the Fourth of July*. Starring Tom Cruise as Ron Kovic, a disabled war veteran, it was one of the first films to take a serious look at the trauma of veterans, including those who had been injured and were trying to adapt to society on the home front.

ERA OF THE ACTION HERO

In keeping with a hard-line approach toward the Soviet Union, the Reagan years saw a steady stream of macho heroes on movie screens, with men firing giant weapons while spitting out manly, quotable one-liners. Perhaps the best-known and biggest star of the decade was Sylvester Stallone. After writing and starring in *Rocky* (a film about a down-and-out boxer who gets a shot at the heavyweight championship), Stallone found renewed fame playing John Rambo, a traumatized Vietnam vet, in the film *First Blood* (1982). In the second film of the popular series, *Rambo: First Blood Part Two* (1985), Rambo returns to North Vietnam and goes on a massive killing spree, freeing American prisoners. These actions were cathartic for a nation still feeling powerless after the failure of the Vietnam War. Two other Rambo films were released in 1988 and 2008. These films also represented a change in political tone. Unlike the earlier films, which were critical of American involvement in Vietnam, the U.S. government is portrayed as heroic in the later films.

Though Sylvester Stallone was the most popular, he was hardly the only macho action star of the 1980s. What follows is a short list of the major stars and the testosterone-driven roles for which they were best known.

Arnold Schwarzenegger—
    The Terminator (1984, 1991, 2003)
Harrison Ford—
    Indiana Jones (1981, 1984, 1989, 2008)
Chuck Norris—
    Missing in Action (1984, 1985)
Bruce Willis—
    Die Hard (1988, 1990, 1995, 2007, 2013)

Mel Gibson—
  Lethal Weapon (1987, 1989, 1992, 1998)
Jean-Claude Van Damme—
  No Retreat, No Surrender (1986) and *Bloodsport* (1988)

Even more traditional movie stars such as Richard Gere and Tom Cruise found success playing super-macho soldiers in *An Officer and a Gentleman* (1982) and *Top Gun* (1986), respectively, both hit films that extolled the glory and might of the U.S. military.

GREED IS GOOD

In October 1987, the U.S. stock market took a major dip. In December of the same year, director Oliver Stone scored with *Wall Street*, a movie that summed up the money-making ethos of the era. Michael Douglas won an Academy Award for his role as Gordon Gekko, a ruthless investment banker who befriends Bud Fox, played by Charlie Sheen, in an effort to take over and dismantle Fox's father's airline. Stone's film cast an extremely critical eye at the tenor of the 1980s, which condoned making money at any cost. Ironically, while Stone conceived Gekko as a character to be despised, audiences embraced him. In fact, a modification of one of Gekko's most famous lines became the tagline for a generation of aspiring investment bankers and brokers: "Greed is good." A sequel, *Wall Street: Money Never Sleeps*, was released in 2010, but it was not nearly the success the film industry expected it would be. Amidst the fallout from the 2008 bank bailout and the Bernie Madoff Ponzi-scheme scandal, it seemed that greed was no longer good.

THE BATTLE OF THE SEXES

If relationships in the 1970s were marked by such films as Woody Allen's *Annie Hall*, films of the 1980s continued to reflect an increased openness about love and sex. In 1982, Dustin Hoffman played a frustrated actor who finally lands a meaty role, but only when he dresses up as a woman. *Tootsie* used comedy to highlight the ways in which men mistreat women and the ways in which women let that mistreatment continue. Hoffman's character's time pretending to be a woman teaches him how to be a better man. The same year, Blake Edwards directed *Victor Victoria*, another hit whose plot revolved around a character's need to cross-dress in order to find fame. In this case, Julie Andrews plays a woman named Victoria, but she becomes a star as Victor. As in *Tootsie*, the story places the characters in situations in which they are forced to see the world from the point of view of the opposite sex. *Victor Victoria* also broke new ground by featuring and accepting openly gay characters and transvestites.

Other movies in the 1980s stood out for their insight into the dynamics of relationships between men and women. Woody Allen's *Hannah and Her Sisters* (1986) brought to life the humor and subtleties among three sisters in Manhattan and their respective, and sometimes overlapping, lovers. In 1987, *Broadcast News* turned sexual politics upside down by telling a story of a young female reporter (played by Holly Hunter) torn between a male bimbo (played by William Hurt) and a smart, but less attractive friend (played by Albert Brooks). Finally, *When Harry Met Sally . . .* (1989), starring Billy Crystal and Meg Ryan, pushed the discussion of differences between male and female viewpoints even further. The movie is filled with humorous dialogue that posits an overarching question: Can a man and a woman ever truly be friends? The following exchange is from one of the opening scenes, as Harry and Sally, who have just met, drive from Chicago to New York City.

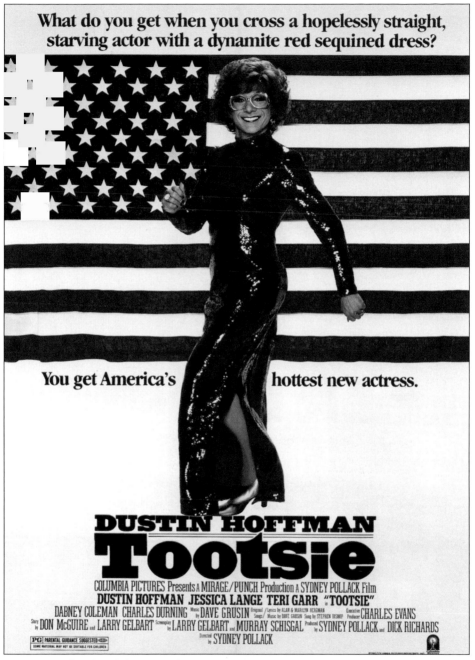

The battle of the sexes is an eternal theme. In *Tootsie*, Dustin Hoffman plays a man who dresses up like a woman to get an acting role and, in the course of that role, learns a thing or two about women.

Harry: What I'm saying . . . is that men and women can't
be friends, because the sex part always gets in the way.

Sally: That's not true. I have a number of men friends
and there's no sex involved.

Harry: No, you don't.

Sally: Yes, I do.

Harry: No, you don't.

Sally: Yes, I do.

Harry: You only think you do.

Sally: You're saying I'm having sex with these men without my knowledge?

Harry: No, I'm saying they all *want* to have sex with you.

When Harry Met Sally . . . is filled with other similar riffs on the differences between men and women, turning the movie into one of the most talked-about films of the decade. It is still frequently shown on TV.

During the 1980s several women made notable professional advancements. In 1981, Ronald Reagan appointed Sandra Day O'Connor to the Supreme Court. She became the first female Supreme Court justice. Three years later, Geraldine Ferraro became the first woman to run for vice president. In Hollywood, more female filmmakers began to make their mark. TV actress Penny Marshall became an A-list director with hits such as *Big* (1988), a film in which Tom Hanks plays a twelve-year-old boy who makes a wish to become "big" and finds himself in his future adult body.

In 1983, Barbara Streisand produced, wrote, directed, and starred in the film adaptation of *Yentl*, a musical set in the early twentieth century. *Yentl* is about a religious Jewish girl who pretends to be a boy so she can go to school. Amy Heckerling became one of Hollywood's most successful directors with hits such as *Fast Times at Ridgemont High* (1982), a quick-paced,

JOHN HUGHES

Though director John Hughes's (1950–2009) film career has included comedies, dramas, and family-oriented fare, he is best remembered for his five high school–set films that captured teenage angst in the mid–1980s.

Pulling from his own experience in high school, Hughes created films filled with uncertainty, apathy, and peer pressure in the lives of teenagers. *Ferris Bueller's Day Off* (1986), *The Breakfast Club* (1985), and *Sixteen Candles* (1984) are now considered to be classic teen films. At the core of these movies are characters who are lonely, feel misunderstood by their parents and peers, and desire nothing more than friendship and understanding. Hughes also portrays high school as miserable, unjust, and boring. In fact, the antagonists in many of his films are teachers or principals who take pleasure in making their students' lives more difficult.

John Hughes had a string of hits in the 1980s, most of them with Molly Ringwald playing the lead, as in this still photo from *The Breakfast Club*.

bawdy spoof of high school life that introduced the country to a host of young stars, including Sean Penn as a perpetually stoned surfer named Jeff Spicoli.

DECADE IN REVIEW

Were the 1980s a low point in American cinema? Perhaps. Still, though the decade may not have produced many hard-hitting, thought-provoking movies, plenty of films stand out from the pack. Written and directed by Barry Levinson, *Diner* (1982) was a highly amusing take on teenage life in Baltimore in the early 1960s. It starred a host of up-and-coming actors, including Kevin Bacon, Mickey Rourke, Paul Reiser, and Ellen Barkin. *Cocoon* (1985) told a poignant story of a group of elderly men and women who find the secret of eternal youth. It was one of the first films directed by Ron Howard (known to many as the child star who played Opie on *The Andy Griffith Show* in the 1960s).

Moonstruck (1987) earned Cher an Academy Award as Best Actress for her portrayal of a young Italian woman who falls in love with her fiancé's younger brother.

ACADEMY AWARD WINNERS OF BEST PICTURE

So as to include all films that are released in a given year for award consideration, the Academy Awards ceremony is held the following year. For example, the awards for the 1980 films were given out in 1981.

1980: *Ordinary People*
The directorial debut of Robert Redford, *Ordinary People*, based on the novel by Judith Guest, follows the disintegration of an upper-middle-class family after the death of their oldest son.

1981: *Chariots of Fire*
Set in the 1920s, *Chariots of Fire* is the story of two deeply religious runners, one the son of Scottish missionaries living in China and the other a Jewish student studying at Cambridge University. Both are accepted as runners for the British team during the 1924 Olympics but must balance their religious and personal convictions with their love of running.

1982: *Gandhi*
Gandhi is the biographical film chronicling the life of Mohandas Gandhi, who led the nonviolent resistance movement to end British colonial rule in India.

1983: *Terms of Endearment*
Based on the novel by Larry McMurtry, *Terms of Endearment* follows the love-hate relationship of Aurora and her daughter Emma from the latter's childhood to her deathbed.

1984: *Amadeus*
Amadeus is a period drama set in Vienna, Austria, in the early 1800s. Antonio Salieri narrates the film from an

insane asylum. It tells the story of his jealousy of the young prodigy Wolfgang Amadeus Mozart and of his ultimately unsuccessful attempt to destroy young Mozart's career.

1985: *Out of Africa*
Loosely based on Karen Blixen's memoir (written under the name Isak Dinesen), *Out of Africa* tells the story of a Danish woman who moves to Africa and finds herself in charge of a coffee plantation.

1986: *Platoon*
Platoon (the first film in director Oliver Stone's Vietnam War trilogy) follows a platoon of soldiers during that war and depicts the moral and ethical dilemmas facing privates and officers involved in the conflict.

1987: *The Last Emperor*
The Last Emperor is a biographical film of the life of Pu Yi, the last emperor of China before the communist coup in 1950.

1988: *Rain Man*
When his father dies, Charlie, a car dealer and a hustler, discovers that his father's fortune has been left to a brother he never knew he had: Raymond, an autistic savant living in an institution. Charlie kidnaps him and the fun begins.

1989: *Driving Miss Daisy*
Based on the off-Broadway play by Alfred Uhry, the plot of *Driving Miss Daisy* spans nearly thirty years and depicts the friendship that develops between Daisy Werthan, a Jewish widow living in Atlanta, and Hoke Colburn, an African American man hired by Daisy's son to be her chauffeur.

FIVE

1990s:
The Independent Years

IN THE 1990S, THE UNITED STATES SUDDENLY lost its longtime enemy. On the heels of a host of land-mark arms control agreements with the Soviet Union, the late 1980s saw a stunning event that most Americans would have never imagined possible: the fall of the Berlin Wall. Since World War II, the city of Berlin in Germany had been divided into two sections. While East Berlin was controlled by the Soviet Union, West Berlin, a democracy, was loyal to the United States and the free countries of Western Europe.

In 1961, tensions between the two sides of the city had grown so intense that the Soviet Union erected a giant wall that divided the city in two. But over the following two decades the Soviet Union struggled economically. In 1985, Mikhail Gorbachev was appointed General Secretary of the Communist Party and embarked on a program of *glasnost* (openness) and *perestroika* (restructuring). A culmination of the new thinking came on November 9, 1989, when the Berlin Wall finally came down, symbolizing the end of the cold war.

After years of worry about the Soviet Union, the United States was suddenly the world's lone superpower. In 1991,

Iraqi dictator Saddam Hussein invaded neighboring Kuwait. U.S. President George H. W. Bush organized an international coalition to defeat Hussein's army. The Gulf War lasted only a few days and was entirely airborne. Its success renewed faith in America's military might. But this renewal of faith in the military did not always extend to the government.

TURNING POINTS IN U.S. HISTORY

With the end of the cold war, American filmmakers began to take a closer and more appraising look at earlier eras. A steady stream of historical movies hit theaters in the 1990s. In contrast to the gung-ho *Rambo* movies of the 1980s, films of the 1990s often took a critical view of events in U.S. history.

In 1991, Oliver Stone directed *JFK*, a three-and-a-half hour reinvestigation of President John F. Kennedy's assassination that took the controversial view that Lee Harvey Oswald had not acted alone. Though most historians disagree with Stone's fictionalized take on the subject, the movie moved people of all political stripes to talk seriously about one of the most shocking events of the century.

The very same year, Kevin Costner, the star of *JFK*, won the 1990 Oscar for Best Director of *Dances with Wolves*. The movie portrayed the plight of a Sioux tribe during the Civil War. Told largely from the perspective of the Sioux, the movie was a far cry from an old-fashioned shoot-'em-up western. Rather, Costner's slow-paced, thoughtful film celebrated the American Indian way of life while placing blame for the Indians' mistreatment squarely on the shoulders of white people.

A demonstrator pounds away at the Berlin Wall as East German border guards look on in November 1989, shortly after the German government declared that people were free to cross over the wall, and shortly before the government itself took down the wall.

**A far cry from the shoot-'em-up westerns of the 1950s and 1960s,
Dances with Wolves told the story from the point of the view of the
American Indians, who were driven off their land.**

Clint Eastwood's *Unforgiven* (1992) looked at the same era,
telling the story of an old gunslinger who is unwillingly drawn
into a final battle. In keeping with the revisionist spirit of the
times, the romance of the old western is turned upside down
as the gunslinger (played by Eastwood) finds no joy at all in his
return to killing. *Unforgiven* is also largely credited with revitaliz-
ing the western. Films such as *Tombstone* (1993), *Legends of the Fall*
(1994), and *Wyatt Earp* (1995) followed in the footsteps of *Unforgiven*, though none quite reached the same level of reception.

One of the most important movies of the decade was Steven Spielberg's *Schindler's List* (1993), the story of one man's heroic efforts to save European Jews during World War II. The huge success of Spielberg's movie jump-started a renewed appraisal of the Holocaust. Tom Hanks won an Academy Award for Best Actor in *Forrest Gump* (1994). The film took a humorous look at the past by cleverly editing famous historical footage into which the main character was inserted (a technique Woody Allen had used in his 1983 film, *Zelig*). Hanks then starred in *Apollo 13* (1995), a heroic retelling of the fateful 1970 Apollo moon launch that nearly ended in disaster. In 1997, Spielberg revisited one of the country's most difficult subjects in *Amistad*, a movie that retold the story of a famous slave revolt.

The most popular film of the decade also revisited the nation's history. Director James Cameron's *Titanic* (1997) told the story of the ill-fated ship by focusing on the fictional, tragic love story of two passengers aboard the ship: a poor stowaway (Leonardo DiCaprio) who falls in love with a rich socialite (Kate Winslet) who is engaged to another man. Filled with stunning special effects, it brought Americans to the movie theaters in droves to experience the sinking of the *Titanic*. It was released in 3-D in the spring of 2012.

The final important historical film of the decade drew on the growing nostalgia for World War II and the so-called "greatest generation." Spielberg's World War II film, *Saving Private Ryan* (1998), stood out for its chillingly realistic depiction of the Battle of Normandy on June 6, 1944, or D-Day. That day, U.S. troops landed on Normandy Beach and reclaimed France from Nazi Germany, which had invaded the country in 1940. It was the beginning of the end for America's enemies, the Axis Powers of Germany, Italy, and Japan.

MIRAMAX AND THE INDEPENDENT FILM MOVEMENT

With the big studios still looking for the next big blockbuster or superhero franchise, the job of producing smaller, more cerebral material fell to independent studios. By the end of the 1990s, most large studios had formed independent divisions that focused on making art-house movies. These movies worked on smaller budgets and often could not afford Hollywood stars unless the star agreed to work for a fraction of his or her usual salary. The IFP Independent Spirit Awards were founded in 1984 to honor films that dared "to challenge the status quo." But independent films didn't really catch on with audiences until the 1990s with the formation of Miramax by Harvey and Bob Weinstein.

During the 1990s, Miramax produced a series of small, high-quality films that also caught on with the public and made money. Miramax first made a name for itself by producing art and foreign-language films that other studios wouldn't consider. Some of their early triumphs included Italy's *Cinema Paradiso* (1988), which won Best Foreign Language Film at the Oscars, and Steven Soderbergh's groundbreaking *Sex, Lies and Videotape* (1989). After that, many of the best and most award-winning films of the decade came from the small studio.

Beginning with *The Crying Game* in 1992, Miramax had an eleven-year streak of movies that were nominated for Best Picture at the Academy Awards. In 1993, the Walt Disney Company bought Miramax, but allowed the Weinsteins to remain in charge and gave them a considerable amount of freedom. The company's enormous success is a testament to Miramax's ability to choose high-quality projects at a time when mainstream studios focused on making action and adventure pictures with highly paid stars. That Miramax's films found popularity in the same market as such movies as Spielberg's rollicking dinosaur adventure, *Jurassic Park* (1993), shows that while Americans sometimes wanted to sit back and enjoy themselves, they also welcomed stories filled with greater complexity. Miramax was not the only maker of independent films, but its remarkable successes made both the public and producers more receptive to independent film.

One of the most successful Miramax films of the 1990s did feature big-name stars. Quentin Tarantino's *Pulp Fiction* (1994) starred John Travolta and Samuel L. Jackson as hit men who, between murders, chat casually about everything from philosophy to French fast food. *Pulp Fiction*, perhaps the most groundbreaking movie of the 1990s, brought the viewer into a disturbing world of drug lords, crooks, and drifters in Los Angeles. A movie without a traditional plot, the story unfolds out of order, beginning and ending with the same robbery. Fascinating for its philosophical bent and disturbing to many in its casual depiction of violence, *Pulp Fiction* set a new tone in American cinema.

Another major factor in the success of the independent film industry is Robert Redford's Sundance Film Festival, which takes place in January of each year in Utah. Founded in 1978, the festival has helped introduce many prolific directors, such as Steven Soderbergh, Quentin Tarantino, Darren Aronofsky, and Jim Jarmusch, to film critics and film studio executives. Studios will sometimes buy the distribution rights to independent films during festivals so that these films can be shown to larger, more mainstream audiences. Nine of the films shown at the 2010 festival went on to receive Academy Award nominations, and four of the five Academy Award nominees for Best Documentary had been screened at Sundance.

In this scene from Quentin Tarantino's genre-busting film, *Pulp Fiction*, John Travolta, who plays a gun for hire, takes to the dance floor with Uma Thurman, who plays his jealous boss's reckless wife.

THE DECADE OF THE SURPRISE ENDING

One of the biggest hits of the decade was writer and director M. Night Shyamalan's *The Sixth Sense* (1999), a psychological thriller about a nine-year-old boy who sees ghosts (famously saying, "I see dead people"). The boy shares his experiences with a therapist played by Bruce Willis. *The Sixth Sense* made a splash, in part due to a great surprise ending. It seemed that *The Sixth Sense* was following a trend. Four other excellent films of the decade, *The Crying Game* (1992), *Se7en* (1995), *The Usual Suspects* (1995), and *Fight Club* (1999), also featured some sort of surprise twist or ending.

WOMEN AND GAY RIGHTS

The early 1990s saw several films that spoke volumes about a swelling anger in American society over the treatment of women and homosexuals. One of the most significant films of the decade was *Thelma & Louise* (1991), written by Callie Khouri and starring Susan Sarandon and Geena Davis. As the movie opens, the two women are ready to take a weekend vacation, despite the fact that Thelma's husband won't let her go. They outsmart Thelma's husband and go anyway. Soon after, Thelma is nearly raped at a rest stop. Louise shoots the man and the two friends are forced to flee.

Chased by the police, Thelma and Louise go on a crime spree across the south trying to make it to Mexico and freedom. Finally cornered, the two friends decide that they can't go back to a society where women are so poorly treated, and they drive off a cliff to their deaths. A movie that takes a stark look at the casual abuse suffered by many women, *Thelma & Louise* was in perfect step with its time.

Penny Marshall's *A League of Their Own* (1992) told the story of the female professional baseball league that was formed during World War II when most young male athletes were fighting overseas. One of the most notable comedies of the decade was *Groundhog Day* (1993), starring Bill Murray as Phil, an extremely obnoxious weatherman. Phil is forced to repeat the same day over and over again, slowly learning to become a better person and earn the affection of a woman, Rita (played by Andie MacDowell). Another great comedy of the decade was the British movie *Four Weddings and a Funeral* (1994), which applied Woody Allen–like neuroses to a young man (played by Hugh Grant) searching for the meaning of love. The movie was an ensemble piece that highlighted a new trend in modern urban life: for many young, independent, single people, their friends became their family.

Philadelphia, released in 1993, was the first popular Hollywood film to focus squarely on the AIDS crisis. Tom Hanks won an Academy Award for his portrayal of Andrew Beckett, a gay attorney who is diagnosed with AIDS. He is fired from his law firm when the other partners learn of his condition. Beckett hires a lawyer, played by Denzel Washington, to defend him in a suit against his firm. Along with highlighting the ravages of a dreadful disease, *Philadelphia* told Americans that gay men deserve to be treated as equal members of society. In 1999, Vermont became the first U.S. state to allow civil unions between men and women of the same sex. At the time, the law outraged much of the nation. Today, nine states accept same-sex civil unions, and nine states and the District of Columbia allow same-sex marriage. *Philadelphia* was also important in its casting of Washington as an attorney. This role opened doors for African American actors looking to play leading parts that had traditionally been thought of as white roles.

THE RISE OF ANIMATED FILMS

Though the Walt Disney Company had been producing animated films since the late 1920s, they reached a new level of success in 1991 when the Disney adaptation of the French film *Beauty and the Beast* won Best Motion Picture Comedy or Musical at the Golden Globe Awards and was nominated for Best Picture at the Academy Awards—the first animated film to receive the honor. Throughout the 1990s, Disney continued to produce critically acclaimed animated films, including *Aladdin* (1992), *The Lion King* (1994), and *Mulan* (1998).

Disney's *Beauty and the Beast* was the first animated film to be nominated for a Best Picture Oscar, and it sparked the rise of the genre.

However, Disney was no longer the only animated powerhouse in the market. The computer graphics and hardware company Pixar had developed new technology for animation. Pixar partnered with Walt Disney Feature Animation to create *Toy Story* (1995), the first computer-animated feature-length film. After the critical and box-office success of the film, Pixar and Disney went on to produce other very successful films, including two *Toy Story* sequels (1999, 2010), *A Bug's Life* (1998), *Monsters Inc.* (2001), *Finding Nemo* (2003), *WALL-E* (2008), and *Up* (2009). Almost every film Pixar has released has been nominated for at least one Academy Award, and both *Up* and *Toy Story 3* were nominated for Best Picture.

In 2006, Pixar became a Disney company, giving Disney more hold on the animated-film market. However, other computer-animation companies, most notably Dreamworks Animation, the studio behind *Shrek* (2001), *Wallace & Gromit* (2005), *Kung Fu Panda* (2008), and *How to Train Your Dragon* (2010), have also received much critical acclaim. In the twenty-first century, animated features would rank among the most profitable, innovative, and entertaining films produced.

THE DECADE IN REVIEW

During the 1990s, film attendance was up. Many Hollywood studios still believed that high-budget films with big stars, explosive action scenes, and wild special effects would reap large dividends—often, they were right. Even so, audiences also enjoyed darker dramas. In 1996, *Jerry Maguire*, a film starring Tom Cruise as a sports agent, was the only film nominated for Best Picture at the Academy Awards that did not come from an independent studio.

As Americans continued to go to the movies, the Internet and DVD players allowed people to watch movies at home with greater ease than before. In the late 1980s, approximately 450 to 500 films were released each year in theaters. This was the same number of films as were released during the Golden Age of Hollywood in the 1930s and 1940s, when studios contracted actors to work exclusively for them and star in a certain number of films per year.

But by the 1990s, about 40 percent of all films went straight to video. The time between a movie's release and its availability on DVD was becoming much shorter as well. A movie might run in the theaters for a month or so, then be available at a video or DVD rental store nine months later—a far cry from the early 1970s when a moviegoer could only see a film when it was in the theater. Suddenly, anyone with a VCR or DVD player and a television could watch almost any movie they wanted in the privacy of their living room. By the end of the 1990s, most movies were being released on DVD. The varied ways to see movies would only grow in the coming decade.

ACADEMY AWARD WINNERS FOR BEST PICTURE

So as to include all films that are released in a given year for award consideration, the Academy Awards ceremony is held the following year. For example, the awards for the 1990 films were given out in 1991.

1990: *Dances with Wolves*
The film adaptation of a novel by Michael Blake, *Dances with Wolves* is set during the Civil War. It centers on a Union army lieutenant who travels to the frontier in search of a military post, and the relationship he develops with the Lakota Indians. Much of the dialogue is in Lakota and subtitled in English.

1991: *The Silence of the Lambs*
The Silence of the Lambs, based on a novel by Thomas Harris, follows FBI trainee Clarice Starling as she befriends the brilliant, imprisoned serial killer Dr. Hannibal Lecter in order to get his help in the search for the identity of "Buffalo Bill," another serial killer.

1992: *Unforgiven*
Set in the Old West, *Unforgiven* tells the story of an aging outlaw who, though he has retired to a life of farming, agrees to take one more job. Clint Eastwood produced, directed, and starred in the film.

1993: *Schindler's List*
Based on the novel *Schindler's Ark* by Thomas Keneally, *Schindler's List* tells the story of a German businessman who saves more than a thousand Polish-Jewish refugees by putting them to work in his factory and shielding them against the Nazis.

1994: *Forrest Gump*

Forrest Gump, based on the novel by Winston Groom, is the story of a slow-witted, gullible man named Forrest Gump who, mostly by coincidence, witnesses some of the defining historical moments of the latter twentieth century.

1995: *Braveheart*

Loosely based on an epic poem from the fifteenth century, *Braveheart* tells the story of Scottish warrior William Wallace, who fought in the First War of Scottish Independence against King Edward I of England. The film is directed by and stars Mel Gibson.

1996: *The English Patient*

Set during World War II, *The English Patient*, based on the novel by Michael Ondaatje, tells the story of a badly burned Hungarian geographer known to his nurse as "the English patient."

1997: *Titanic*

Cowritten, coproduced, directed, and edited by James Cameron, *Titanic* is the love story of two passengers who meet on the ill-fated ship, the *RMS Titanic*.

1998: *Shakespeare in Love*

Shakespeare in Love is the fictionalized story of an affair William Shakespeare had while writing *Romeo and Juliet*.

1999: *American Beauty*

American Beauty is a satire of the typical middle-class family's pursuit of happiness, and what happens when that pursuit is interrupted by the loss of the father's high-paying job.

Pedestrians run from the scene as one of the World Trade Center towers collapses in New York City on September 11, 2001.

2000s:
A Troubled Time

THE DEFINING EVENT OF THE TURN OF THE
new century was tragic. On September 11, 2001, terrorists
attacked the United States by crashing two hijacked planes
into New York City's World Trade Center towers and a third
into the Pentagon in Washington, D.C. A fourth hijacked
plane was taken over by passengers and forced to crash before
hitting its target—the White House. The 9/11 attacks
changed the tone of the country. For a brief time, Americans
stood as one, ready to defeat al-Qaeda, the terrorist network
responsible for the attacks. But soon President George W.
Bush made the decision to invade Iraq, based on information
that its dictator, Saddam Hussein, was harboring weapons
of mass destruction that could be used to attack the United
States. That information turned out to be incorrect, and it
led to a fierce antiwar movement.

In 2005 Hurricane Katrina destroyed much of New
Orleans. Three years later, financial markets crashed, sending
the U.S. economy into a recession. For the first time in years,
unemployment began to skyrocket as companies were forced to
lay off workers they could no longer afford to employ. In 2009,

Barack Obama took office on a wave of optimism and hope for change. Once in office, he faced extremely stiff opposition from the Republican Party. The movies of the first decade of the twenty-first century have reflected the change and turmoil.

During the first ten years of the new century, Hollywood continued to churn out crowd-pleasing blockbusters such as *The Da Vinci Code* (2006), based on Dan Brown's smash hit book of the same name, as well as film versions of popular super-hero comics, such as *X-Men* (2000), *Spider-Man* (2002), *Batman Begins* (2005), and *Iron Man* (2008). These films have, at times, reinforced the image of the United States as a strong terrorist-fighting state. Other movies dealt with the issues of economic insecurity that plagued the country later in the decade.

Comic books turned cinematic have turned into big business for Hollywood studios, as hits such as *Iron Man*, based on the Marvel comics character, spawn sequels and spinoffs.

THE IRAQ WAR

President George W. Bush's most controversial decision during his eight years in office was to invade Iraq in 2003. The initial invasion was a stunning success. U.S. troops rolled into Baghdad and took control of the county in a matter of days. However, the aftermath was very difficult. With no solid plan about how to govern the country, U.S. soldiers struggled to keep the peace between rival terrorist groups. At the same time, U.S. officials found it extremely difficult to set up a new Iraqi government. The U.S. did not end its involvement in Iraq until December 2011.

On top of these problems, investigations of the Iraq countryside turned up no evidence that Saddam Hussein had weapons of mass destruction, a discovery that undercut the stated purpose of the invasion. Conservatives continued to support the war, arguing that a free Iraq would encourage other democracies in the region. However, most of the films about the war—largely made by liberal filmmakers—took a darker view of the conflict.

While Ridley Scott's *Black Hawk Down* (2001) was released only a few months after 9/11 and before the U.S. invasion of Iraq, it captured the tension surrounding a failed helicopter mission in Somalia, a notable U.S. foreign policy misstep. But the first 9/11 feature from Hollywood was Paul Greengrass's *United 93* (2006), a retelling of the hijacked flight that a group of brave passengers forced to crash before it could hit its target in Washington D.C. The same year, Oliver Stone directed *World Trade Center*, a movie that told the story of two police officers who were among the last rescue workers to be pulled from the fallen World Trade Center towers. Perhaps the most successful film to come out of the 9/11 tragedy was the 2009 Academy Award winner for Best Picture, *The Hurt Locker*, an intense look at U.S. soldiers in Iraq whose job it is to defuse roadside bombs.

In what would be a return to the antiwar sentiment of the 1970s, movies such as *Black Hawk Down* highlighted the ugly side of war rather than its heroism.

Yet, many of these and other 9/11–related films failed at the box office. Historically, the most successful movies having to do with a particular conflict usually appear a decade or so after it is over. For example, the highly successful *Platoon* came out in 1987, twelve years after the fall of Saigon. Moviegoers typically do not flock to realistic wartime dramas when the realities of war are still fresh in their lives. This is especially true in modern times when people can see war footage on the nightly news.

GOOD VS. EVIL

The biggest films of the early part of the decade, both at the box office and at awards ceremonies, were Peter Jackson's film adaptations of J. R. R. Tolkien's *The Lord of the Rings* trilogy. These epic films told of a small hobbit's effort to free Middle Earth from the evils of Sauron. All three films, *The Lord of the Rings: The Fellowship of the Ring* (2001), *The Lord of the Rings: The Two Towers* (2002), and *The Lord of the Rings: The Return of the King* (2003), were giant hits. The acting and direction of these films were exceptional, and so were the many stunning special effects. *The Lord of the Rings* also reassured an anxious nation and world that evil could be defeated against impossible odds.

James Cameron's *Avatar* came to the screens in 2009. It was another epic film in which good triumphs over evil. Using 3-D and cutting-edge film technology, Cameron created an entirely new visual experience for filmgoers. *Avatar* told the story of a U.S. Marine's heroic efforts to save the alien Na'vi tribe from extermination. Visually spectacular, *Avatar* went on to become the largest-grossing film in history.

HARD TIMES AND LIBERAL OUTRAGE

One of the biggest stars of the early twenty-first century was George Clooney, an actor who gained attention by playing

The three *Lord of the Rings* movies, adapted from J. R. R. Tolkien's book trilogy, were a return to the idea that good conquers evil. The movies were megahits.

morally compromised middle-aged men. In 2009, Clooney starred in Jason Reitman's *Up in the Air* as Ryan Bingham, a man whose job is to travel around the country firing employees for companies that do not want to deal with the emotionally taxing task of firing their own employees. In the wake of rising unemployment and the U.S. banking crisis of 2008, *Up in the Air* was a movie in perfect step with the economic and emotional climate. It exposed the soullessness at the core of many large corporations.

Documentary filmmaker Michael Moore rose to prominence with a series of movies that took a critical look at U.S. institutions. In the wake of the tragic shootings at Columbine

High School in Colorado, Moore released *Bowling for Columbine* in 2002. This documentary film took on the gun lobby and argued for gun control in a grimly comedic way. It questioned, for instance, why banks sometimes give away guns as incentives for opening checking accounts. Two years later, Moore's *Fahrenheit 9/11* (2004) took a scathing look at the political mistakes and miscalculations that led to the second war in Iraq. Because of its overtly negative view of the Bush Administration, Disney, which produced the film, initially refused to release it—a move that ultimately added to the film's success. In time, Moore's film made such an impression on the American public that Arizona Senator John McCain called the documentarian a "disingenuous filmmaker," or, a liar, during the 2004 Republican Convention, which Moore attended.

Another important documentary film of the decade was made by former vice president Al Gore. After losing the 2000 presidential election to George W. Bush in a decision legislated by the Supreme Court, Gore devoted his career to spreading the word about the perils of climate change. His movie about global warming, *An Inconvenient Truth* (2006), touched a deep chord with many Americans.

GAY RIGHTS

One of the most important movies of the decade was *Brokeback Mountain* (2005), which told the story of the love affair between two cowboys, played by Heath Ledger and Jake Gyllenhaal. Despite its poignancy and fine acting, it's hard to imagine that such a film would have been popular in an earlier era. But in a decade where gay characters appeared on many TV shows and the U.S. government would soon repeal "Don't Ask Don't Tell," *Brokeback Mountain* was a hit that earned eight Oscar nominations.

ALPHA WOMEN AND BETA MALES

When Sofia Coppola (daughter of famed director Francis Ford Coppola) was nominated for Best Director for her 2003 movie *Lost in Translation*, she became the third woman (and the first American woman) ever to earn a nomination in the category. At the same time that women were being afforded greater

When Sofia Coppola was nominated for Best Director for her 2003 movie *Lost in Translation*, she was the first American woman ever to be nominated in that category. Shown here are Bill Murray and Scarlett Johansson, who starred in the film.

professional respect in Hollywood, female audiences drove the box office for much of the decade.

After directing several critically acclaimed independent films, Catherine Hardwicke chose to direct the first of the five *Twilight* films. A vampire romance based on Stephenie Meyer's wildly popular young adult book series, *Twilight* (2008) earned $70.6 million in its opening weekend, making Hardwicke the first female director to successfully launch a film franchise. Seventy-five percent of *Twilight*'s audience was female.

The market for films with female leads continued with the first of the two movies based on the long-running *Sex and the City* television series. *Sex and the City* (2008) and *Sex and the City 2* (2010) cashed in on the fan base of the popular TV show. Women went en masse to the first *Sex and the City* movie and even threw parties centered on the film. *Sex and the City 2*, however, bombed with critics and crashed at the box office. By 2010, the moment for excessive spending on shoes and booze may have passed. Also, the second film, set in Dubai, was much campier than both the television series and the first film.

Capping a decade in which women were finally getting their due in Hollywood, Kathryn Bigelow became the first woman to win the Oscar for Best Director for *The Hurt Locker*. Many people were shocked that she won for this small, independent film over James Cameron (Bigelow's ex-husband) for his direction of *Avatar*.

The 2000s were also marked by a new kind of male hero: the beta male. In a series of successful comedies, producer-director Judd Apatow introduced the comically hapless slacker in desperate need of a woman's care and attention. In 2005, Apatow's *The 40-Year-Old Virgin* came out. The film centers on a middle-aged man-child (played by Steve Carrell) who has never had sex. Carrell is finally able to grow up through the love of a mature woman.

The big surprise of Judd Apatow's surprisingly sweet movie, *The 40-Year-Old Virgin*, is that the virgin of the title is male.

In 2007, Apatow released *Knocked Up*, the story of an unemployed, pot-smoking slacker (played by Seth Rogen) who slowly matures when faced with the prospect of fatherhood. In these and many other comedies of the decade, men are portrayed as humorous screw-ups.

One of the biggest hits of 2009 was *The Hangover*, a comedy about the amusing, though highly infantile, adventures of male friends at a bachelor party in Las Vegas. Though not an

Until *Twilight*, blockbusters were traditionally aimed at a male audience. With an audience that was 75 percent female, this film franchise proved that women could also drive mega–box office.

97

Apatow film, *The Hangover* profited from the success of the character archetypes Apatow's films had ushered into prominence. Indeed, during the first decade of the 2000s, perhaps more than ever in film history, it was the women who were most often the grown-ups.

RELIGION IN PUBLIC LIFE

Actor-turned-director Mel Gibson was at the center of a controversy in 2004 when he released *The Passion of the Christ*, a film that depicted the last twelve hours in Jesus Christ's life in extremely violent and grisly terms. Fans of the movie and many Christians appreciated Gibson's honest portrayal of the pain Jesus endured near the end. Others objected loudly to the excessive violence and what they considered its alleged anti-Semitic bias. As with many films, the controversy led to great box office revenue. *The Passion of the Christ* was a big hit that got the American people talking about religion's place in society.

LOOKING FORWARD

Moviegoers face a future with almost unlimited options. Netflix, Hulu, and many other websites are devoted to bringing movies directly to users' computers, televisions, and smartphones. Some of these sites offer some content for free, while others offer content to subscribers. At the same time, if a

Social media and the Internet have changed the way we live, and the way we watch movies. Not surprisingly, perhaps, *The Social Network*, about the rise of Facebook, was one of the most successful movies of 2010.

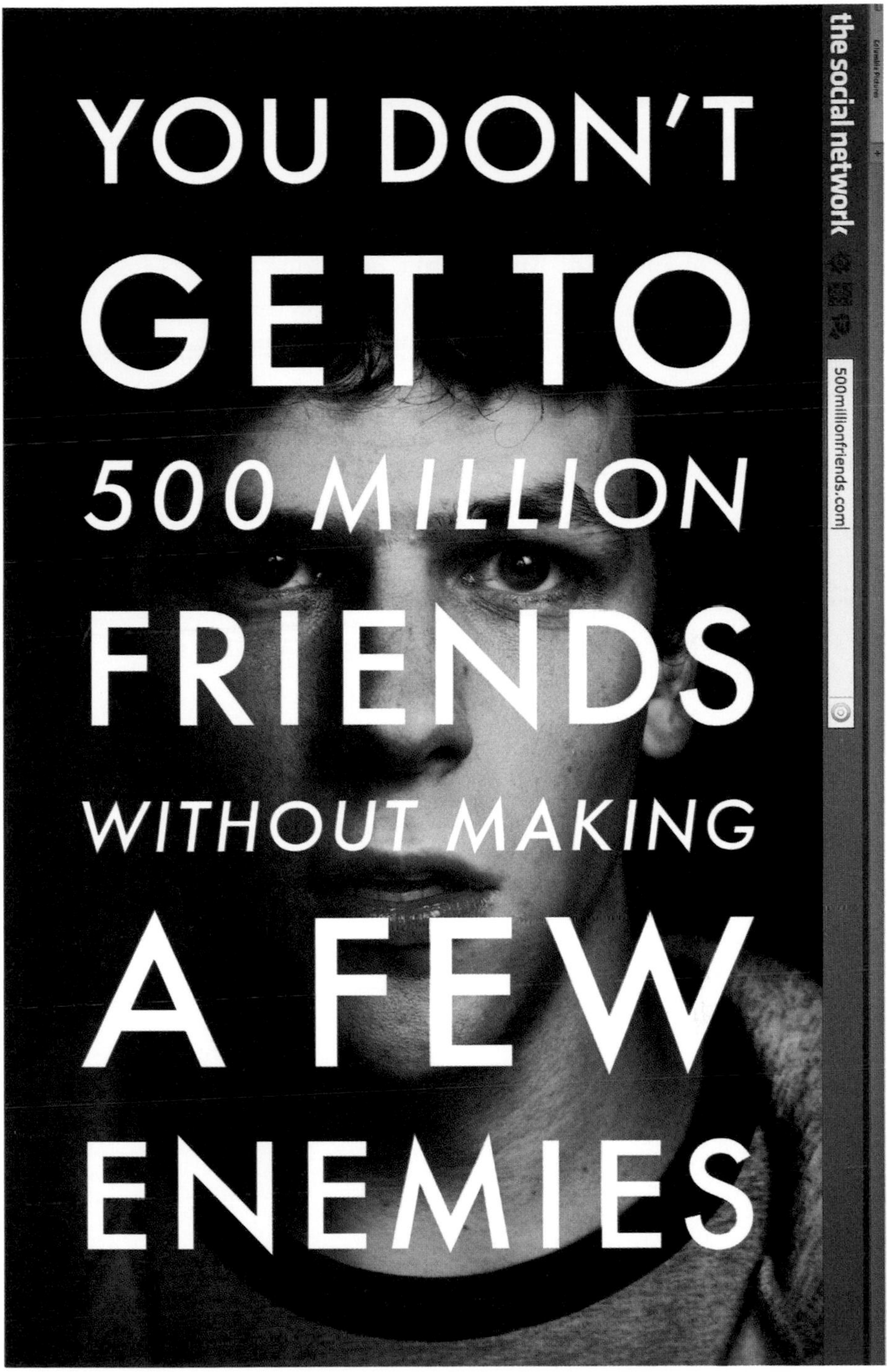
YOU DON'T
GET TO
500 MILLION
FRIENDS
WITHOUT MAKING
A FEW
ENEMIES
the social network
500millionfriends.com

viewer misses a movie in the theater, he or she can often see it soon after "On Demand" on their televisions or by renting or streaming a DVD. Movie advertising has changed, too, as more and more people spend their days logged onto sites like Facebook. One hugely successful film of the decade was *The Social Network* (2010), a retelling of the drama involved in the creation of Facebook, based on the nonfiction book *The Accidental Billionaires*, written by Ben Mezrich on the same topic.

So where does this leave production studios? Still in the driver's seat. Though television, books, and other media still have a lot to say in commenting on the culture of the times, movies have the most influence—and not just in the United States. James Cameron's *Avatar* was an international phenomenon. With more ways to distribute films across the globe, it seems certain that movies will continue to have a lot to say about what society is thinking and feeling for generations to come.

ACADEMY AWARD NOMINEES FOR BEST PICTURE

So as to include all films that are released in a given year for award consideration, the Academy Awards ceremony is held the following year. For example, the awards for the 2000 films were given out in 2001.

2000: *Gladiator*
Set in the second century CE, *Gladiator* tells the story of the rise and fall of Maximus, a prominent Roman general who, after an assassination attempt, becomes a Roman gladiator.

2001: *A Beautiful Mind*
Based on the life of John Nash, a Nobel Laureate in Economics, *A Beautiful Mind* tells the story of a brilliant man who was also a paranoid schizophrenic.

2002: *Chicago*
The film adaptation of the Broadway musical, *Chicago* is about imprisoned female murderers in the 1920s and their ploys to manipulate the media in their favor to avoid execution.

2003: *The Lord of the Rings: The Return of the King*
The last film in Peter Jackson's trilogy, *The Lord of the Rings: The Return of the King* tells of an epic battle waged by those helping Frodo destroy the ring.

2004: *Million Dollar Baby*
The story of a hard-nosed boxing trainer and a promising female boxer he agrees to coach, *Million Dollar Baby*, based on short stories by F. X. Toole, is a sports film with an uncharacteristically tragic ending.

2005: *Crash*

This ensemble film features characters whose lives intertwine over two days in Los Angeles. It highlights social and racial tensions between people of different ethnic and socioeconomic classes. Written, directed, and produced by Paul Haggis, the story is based on an experience he had in 1991 when his Porsche was carjacked.

2006: *The Departed*

The Departed, a crime thriller set in Boston, is based on the Hong Kong film *Infernal Affairs*. It tells the story of two state police officers, one an informant for the Irish mob boss who essentially raised him and the other an undercover officer placed in the mob by the state police.

2007: *No Country for Old Men*

Based on the novel by Cormac McCarthy, *No Country for Old Men* tells the bleak story of a man who is hunted down after he takes $2 million from a crime scene.

2008: *Slumdog Millionaire*

The film adaptation of the novel *Q & A* by Vikas Swarup, *Slumdog Millionaire* is the story of a young man who grew up in the slums of Mumbai and becomes a contestant on the Indian version of *Who Wants to Be a Millionaire?* His success on the show rouses the suspicions of the game show host and law enforcement authorities, and before he can answer the last question, he is detained and questioned about whether or not he is cheating.

2009: *The Hurt Locker*

Set in Baghdad during the Iraq War, *The Hurt Locker* tells the tension-filled story of a three-man U.S. Army Explosive Ordnance Disposal Team whose job it is to disarm bombs.

Notes

CHAPTER THREE

p. 48, "It was great seeing Annie again . . ." Woody Allen and Marshall Brickman, *Annie Hall*. www.imdb.com/title/tt0075686/quotes

CHAPTER FOUR

p. 65, "*What I'm saying . . .*"; Nora Ephron, *When Harry Met Sally . . .* New York: Knopf, 1996, p. 14.

Further Information

BOOKS

O'Brien, Lisa. *Lights, Camera, Action: Making Movies and TV from the Inside Out*. New York: Maple Tree Press, 2007.

Osborne, Robert. *TCM Classic Movie Trivia*. San Francisco: Chronicle Books, 2011.

Schneider, Steven J., ed. *1001 Movies You Must See Before You Die*, 4th Ed. New York: Barron's Educational Series, 2011.

DVDS

Moguls & Movie Stars: A History of Hollywood. Warner Home Video, 2011.

WEBSITES

AMC film site
www.filmsite.org/filmh.html
History of movies by decade, including detailed lists of best movies, Oscar winners, and famous quotes.

History on Film
www.historyonfilm.com
A website of articles about historical movies.

Movie History Timeline
www.infoplease.com/ipea/A0150210.html
A detailed timeline, listing the most important events in the history of motion pictures from the late 1800s to the present.

Bibliography

BOOKS

Biskind, Peter. *Down and Dirty Pictures: Miramax, Sundance and the Rise of Independent Film*. New York: Simon & Schuster, 2004.

Bona, Damien. *Inside Oscar 2*. New York: Ballantine Publishing, 2002.

Goldman, Eric. *The Crucial Decade and After: America, 1945–1960*. New York: Random House, 1960.

Goldman, William. *Adventures in the Screen Trade*. New York: Warner Communications Company, 1983.

Haines, Richard W. *The Moviegoing Experience, 1968–2001*. Jefferson, North Carolina: McFarland & Co., Inc., 2003.

Manchester, William. *The Glory and the Dream*. New York: Bantam Books, 1975.

Schneider, Steven J., ed. *1001 Movies You Must See Before You Die*. New York: Quintet Publishing Limited, 2003.

Wood, Robin. *Hollywood from Vietnam to Reagan . . . and Beyond*. New York: Columbia University Press, 2003

INTERVIEWS

Damien Bona, author of *Inside Oscar 2*. New York: Ballantine Books, 2002.

Index

About the Author

DANIEL BENJAMIN is the author of numerous non-fiction books for young readers. His most recent titles are *Extreme Mountain Biking, Extreme Snow Boarding,* and *Extreme Rock Climbing* for the Sports on the Edge! series. Daniel Benjamin lives in New York City with his wife and two children.